How do you
PLACES IN CORNWALL

Location - Pronunciation - Meaning

by

June Lander

ACANTHUS BOOKS

Published by Acanthus Books, Lanner, Redruth, Cornwall.
TR16 6BS   01209 -.217557

British Library Cataloguing in Publication Data
ISBN 0-9506765-3-5

Printed by Martyn Kimmins Print, St.Agnes

Acknowledgments and Thanks: I owe a great debt to the works written about Cornish names and their derivations - especially those by Oliver Padel of the Institute of Cornish Studies, Craig Weatherhill, T.F.G.Dexter, Julyan Holmes and P.A.S.Pool. Those wanting further expert information should refer to the bibliography at the end.

My thanks go to all those people who have helped with the pronunciation of names in the areas in which they live or were born. These include especially Barbara Olds, Trevor Thomas, Charles Spicer, Hope Blundell, Jim Hosking and Jean Nankervis,as well as the following members and friends of Old Cornwall Societies throughout the county - Peter Askett, Mrs Barrett, Mrs V Bennallick, Wella Brown, Dr. Ken George, Joyce Greenham, Stanley Grenfell, Joyce Hambly, Denis Lusby, Martin Matthews, Mrs L Opie, Margaret Pierce, Mrs G Rundle, John Neal and Mrs J.Zimber.

Finally my thanks to Terry Knight of the Cornish Studies Library and his staff for their expertise and assistance.

May, 2003.

Contents

For
STEVE & NOEL

Who made it all possible

Illustrations

The illustrations include houses of famous Cornish men and women, or of famous people associated with Cornwall.

Front Cover

By Roy Billingham of Lanner, is of Angrouse, Mullion. This 17C thatched house was the home of Thomas and Ursula Triggs, the first leaders of Methodism in Mullion, who were hosts to John Wesley on his travels in Cornwall. A stone in the adjoining field marks Wesley's preaching place. Subsequent owners have included Frank and Veronica Chesher, authors of "The Cornishman's House". The name Angrouse (an grows) means a cross,and could derive from a stone cross which once marked the churchway path from this end of the parish.

The line drawings throughout the text are by Fred Splatt of Camborne. Fred unfortunately died before this book was published, as he was looking forward to seeing his work in print. A Cornishman born at Trevenen Bal, near Helston, Fred was known for his musical and sporting contributions to the community. He was a member of the Holman Climax Male Voice Choir, a founder member of Camborne Music Festival and its secretary for seven years, as well as being a football referee and cricket umpire. He took up art in his later years,and one of his proudest moments was when his painting of Camborne Library was presented to the Queen by Camborne Town Council.

THE LURE OF CORNWALL

Those who love Cornwall fall into several categories - the indigenous Cornish whose families have lived here for centuries; those who have married into Cornish families; the people from other parts who have come to live here - and the millions of visitors who come every year, either for the first time or as a lifelong addiction.

Cornwall has a multitude of attractions, both inland and by the sea, but it is its distinctiveness which is the key factor, highlighted by the almost foreign sounding names found everywhere.

People are intrigued by those names and many would like to know how to say them correctly, and also to find out what they mean.

This little book has been produced in an effort to help them, as well as to pinpoint the location of the main places in Cornwall, both large and small. I have obviously not been able to list every place in Cornwall - that would run to thousands of entries, but if you think I have missed any of real importance, please let me know.

I have also included a short description of the amenities and attractions of places of any size, together with local churches (mainly Church of England, because to cover all the churches and chapels of other denominations in Cornwall would require extensive research), holy wells, a selection of Cornish crosses and ancient monuments, art galleries and places of interest.

However, I have no doubt, that the pronunciation and meanings of the names will probably generate some lively controversy, as there are many inherent difficulties.

PRONUNCIATION

Cornish names are full of richness, and anyone interested in words could not fail to react to such examples as Halzephron, Pigeon Ogo and Marazanvose. As well as being intrigued by these beguiling names, visitors to Cornwall - or even those who have lived here for many years - are often baffled by how to pronounce them.

For instance Delabole, near Camelford, can be a puzzle. It often comes out as 'De'lab'o'lee' when it should be Del'a'BOWL with the accent on the last syllable (not too heavily!). Mousehole, in West Penwith, tends to be pronounced as it looks, but is locally called 'Mow'sl'. I have also heard Mabe, near Falmouth, called 'May'be' and Porthleven, near Helston, called 'Port Eleven.'

The Cornish smile, but, like the inhabitants of other countries, are pleased if you make the effort to find how to say the names correctly.

I have also attempted this work because I am fascinated by Cornwall and its history, and hope in some small way to help in the retention of its heritage.

The area is one of the fastest growing regions as far as population is concerned, and this means many newcomers are not familiar with the Cornish pronunciation. There is too a growing trend for the incomers pronunciation to take precedence. This has happened, for instance, at Wadebridge where the original pronunciation was Wade'BRIDGE but is now almost universally called 'Wadebridge'.

Another typical example of how a name can be changed is that of the Lost Gardens of Heligan. Almost from the time it was first put on the map by Tim Smit it was called Heligan (Helly'gan), with no emphasis on any part of the word. Archie Smith, a retired headmaster living at Gorran Haven, began a correspondence in the Western Morning News in the summer of 2002 saying the correct pronunciation was Hel'IG'un, with the emphasis on the second syllable, and he was backed up by other Cornish writers. His pronunciation has also been confirmed by the Tremayne family who have owned the estate for generations.

One 'foreigner' wrote asking forgiveness for getting it wrong, and added that her birthplace in Lancashire "is spelt and looks like Scar-is-brick, but is pronounced Scares-brick!"

LOCAL DIFFERENCES

The difficulty has been that sometimes Cornish people from the same area can not agree on how some places are pronounced - and even in the same village there are differences of opinion. Breage near Helston being the classic example, with both BREEGE and BRAYGE claimed as correct.

Martin Matthews, former curator of the Helston Museum, who is also President of the Helston Old Cornwall Society and a true Cornishman, told me the older pronunciation was Brayg, but that Breeg had now become more common.

I found many instances of this change from the older ways of pronouncing names, and one wonders how much the infiltration of newcomers over the years has had an influence. Archie Smith told me that his family had lived in the village of Gorran Haven for 300 to 400 years, but now because of the influx of new people he sometimes felt "like a stranger in his own parish".

Other examples of changes include Golitha Falls, near Liskeard, which is now commonly called Go'LY'tha, whereas the older pronunciation, I am told, is Go'LEETH'a.

Launceston, the ancient capital of Cornwall, is now usually pronounced Lawn'son, but Cornish people call it Lan'son. Coverack on The Lizard should be KUV'rek and not COV'er'ack.

Christine North, the Cornwall County Records Officer for many years, told me that Trewarthenick, near Tregony, used to be pronounced by her grandmother as Tr'DIN'ick, whereas she herself would pronounce it Tr'THEN'ick. The unwary, of course, would pronounce it as 'Tree'war'thenick!

This example shows all to clearly the vernacular way of eliding words or running them together. "It's lazy speech", the Secretary of the Newquay Old Cornwall Society, Joyce Greenham, told me.

The older pronunciation can also quite often be traced back historically to the early beginnings of the place and its name, and experts, such as Oliver Padel and Craig Weatherhill, have produced in-depth surveys providing valuable information for scholars and interested amateurs - information is in the bibliography at the end of this publication for those who would like to pursue the subject more thoroughly.

This present book only skims the surface of the matter, but it is hoped that it will arouse the interest of visitors, as well as give residents a slant on places with which they are not particularly familiar.

By consulting local people, as well as members of the Old Cornwall Societies, and trying to produce the right sounds (often phonetically, with the parts of the word to be emphasised in capital letters), I hope to have given the correct pronunciation as near as is possible - but I am open to correction for any future edition.

An example of a local variation was given me by Charles Spicer, who now lives at Carnon Downs, near Truro, but was brought up in Stithians, the well known village lying between Falmouth and Truro. Today most people pronounce this as "Stith'ee'uns". but he told me that when he was a boy it was known as "Stid'ee'uns". Looking at the origin of the name it is interesting to see that it was derived from the dedication of the parish church to Saint Sted'iana.

Cornish, like any other language,has its own rules. Where to put the stress on a name or word can perhaps be best summarised by saying that in two-syllable words the stress is usually on the second one, as in Liskeard (Lis'KARD) and Pendeen (Pen'DEEN).

In words with more than two syllables, the stress is generally on the second part, as in Carvedras (Car'VED'ras').

Having said that, there are many exceptions to the rule - about which even the Cornish themselves don't agree. It is clear, however, that pronunciations are very localised, even down to villages, between two towns, (say Camborne and Redruth), and certainly between areas.

For pronunciation in the St.Buryan area I spoke to local author Jim Hosking. I specially wanted to know how St. Buryan itself was pronounced, as I had been told that "St.Berry'an" was correct (the patron saint being St. Beriana). I had also heard "St. BURRY'an" (to rhyme with hurry) was used - but Jim, who was born in the village, told me that "St. BUR'y'an" (to rhyme with 'fur) is the right way to say it. Now that should get everyone going!

Another interesting instance is the name "Boscawen". This is the family name of the Falmouths, who pronounce it "Bos'CO'en". The family originated at Boscawen in West Penwith, and the local people there also call it "Bos'CO'en". In Truro, however, you will find that most people call the name of the main thoroughfare "Bos'Scorn" Street. The true Truronian also calls Pydar Street 'Py-der' rather than 'Py'dar' Street.

What can be most confusing too is that a word like "ope", meaning a connecting alleyway, is called an "opp" in Truro and "ope" in Falmouth and Redruth. Having written this, I was then told by Barbara Olds, who was brought up in the Truro area and worked in Truro Library for many years, that she says "ope" as well as "opp way"!

Pronouncing the name of a Cornish family called Tregian also poses a problem. Frances Tregian of Golden Manor, near Probus, became famous for sheltering a Catholic priest, Cuthbert Mayne, from the law. He was found and subsequently hung, drawn and quartered at Launceston Goal in the late 16th century. Frances's surname is pronounced "Trudg'un" - which would not be obvious to most people seeing the name for the first time. However, if you drop the "e" from "Tre" and elide that with the rest of the name, one can probably understand how the pronunciation of the name came about.

Another variation, which also has to be borne in mind, is that the county families' way of pronouncing words can be different from the local one (known as "town and gown" in places like Oxford). Lord St. Levan, for instance, pronounces Penzance as Pens'zarns (to rhyme with 'aunts'); while the Graham Vivians pronounce the name of their house Bosahan, near Helford, as "Bs'ayn", while others locally say "Bs'ann".

It is generally acknowledged, however, that more real Cornish names have survived in West Penwith, its wealth being shown in words such as Crows-An-Wra, Men-An-Tol, Woon Gumpus and Zawn Buzz and Gen. The attraction of the area is its ancient history reflected in these wonderful place names.

HISTORY OF THE LANGUAGE

The Celtic language is closely allied to Welsh and Breton, and is descended from the British Language spoken thoughout Britain before the Romans came. During this period, however, many words were borrowed from the Latin, becoming part of the Cornish and Welsh language.

For instance, the word "pont" (a bridge) is the same in Latin, French, Welsh and Cornish; while the English word "harbour", following the same pattern, is portus, port, porth and porth respectively.

Parts of Cornwall were invaded by the English between the 8th and 10th centuries, but Cornish as a language survived until the eighteenth century, and today is spoken by a dedicated band of about three hundred speakers who do not want the language to die out.

It is not surprising, therefore, that there are more Cornish names as you move down the county, with the greatest number still remaining in West Penwith.

ORIGINS AND MEANINGS

As to the meanings, I have consulted many sources including those by T.F.G.Dexter, Piers Dixon, Julyan Holmes, Catherine Rachel John, R.Morton Nance, Oliver Padel, P.A.S.Pool and Christine Truran.

Trying to work out the meaning of a name from its modern form is often difficult. Many which look absolutely obvious turn out to mean something quite different. The earliest available spellings are of great importance - experts have spent years researching this subject, and still admit that there are many names which are obscure or completely unidentifiable; but for more in-depth study please consult the bibliography at the end.

In instances where I have not been able to find a meaning I have put "not known" (ie not known by me!), but would welcome help in this direction.

If there is doubt about a meaning, I have put a question mark after it, and in some cases have put alternative meanings. Again any help over these would also be appreciated.

The old rhyme tells us that "By Tre, Pol and Pen ye shall know Cornishmen".

Certainly these prefixes appear in a great number of Cornish names. By far the most numerous is the use of "Tre" at the beginning of a place name. Tre(or Trev) can mean a farmstead, a settlement, a hamlet or town. In early times "Tre" was added either to the name of a person on the settlement, or to a distinguishing local feature or industry.

For instance, Trelissick, the National Trust garden at Feock, probably means "farm of Ledick" (Tre'ledick - the middle 'd' later changing to an 's'). Whilst Trelan, near St. Keverne, means "farm at a church site" (tre plus lan).

Pol means pool, pond, creek or anchorage, and is found in names such as Polgooth (goose pool) or Polglase (green pool).

Pen means top, head or end, and also headland. Examples are Penpoll, meaning head of the creek ('pen' plus 'poll' creek), and Penrose, end of the moorland ('pen' plus 'ros'moor).

Chy (pronounced 'shy)is also frequently used, meaning a house or building.

Other commonly used word beginnings include Bal(mine); Bos (dwelling or place); Carn (rocks); Coose (woods); Eglos (church); Goon (downs); Hen (ancient); Lan (church site; Men(stone or stones); Nance (valley); Noweth (new); Parc (field); Pons (bridge); Porth (harbour or cove); Treath (beach or seashore); Wartha (above or higher); Wheal (field or mine working); Wollas(lower); and Vean (small).

In his book "Cornish Names" T.F.G.Dexter gives a verse which may help in remembering some common name forms:

> Bod, a home; Pol, a pool,
> Cos, a wood, in summer cool,
> Hal (of doubtful sex), a moor,
> Add Porth, where waves do sometimes roar,
> Next Chy, a house, with hill or Pen
> And all of gender named from men.
> Car, a camp; Goon, a down,
> Kelly, a grove, Tre, a town,
> Ros, a heath; Nans, a vale,
> Lan, a church, all female.

Single nouns include Brea (hill); Gear (fort) or Hayle (estuary).

UNUSUAL NAMES

Unusual names always have a fascination of their own. Who would expect to find Egypt in Cornwall near a place called Jericho, north of Liskeard; Sheffield near Penzance and Barcelona near Looe? For good measure there are places called America, Baltimore, the Bay of Biscay, Bohemia and Flintshire.

Terry Knight, who is in charge of the Cornwall Centre in Redruth, thinks that names like Egypt probably came about when someone visited that country and because they liked it so much, changed their own house name on return to Cornwall. Barcelona, near Pelynt, is mentioned by Geoffrey Grigson in his book "Freedom of the Parish", where he says that the name goes back to at least 1748. "Possibly it was a fancy name bestowed by one of the Trelawns, because in 1637 it was called Trelawne Cross", he said.

Amusing combinations of names include Brandy Wine at Mount Joy in Newquay; Jolly's Bottom at Chacewater; Twizzle Twig at Skinner's Bottom; Little Hell and Trewrong near Par; Paramoor near Hewaswater; Knave Go By at Beacon; Beggar the Boys at Lanyon; Dog Hole Farm at Botus Fleming and Promise Land at St.Agnes. These, and some others, are given in a section at the back of the book in case anyone wants to turn them into a game for children.

Names are an important part of one's life. My husband is continually asked if he is related to Richard Lander, the famous explorer, who is commemorated with a monument at the top of Lemon Street. As far as he knows he is not - but who can tell what he would find if he went far enough back in history?

To me, however, what is more intriguing is that my maiden name of Washford is a Cornish name! Whilst researching for this publication I came across a place called Trewashford near Pillaton - so perhaps I too can claim to have Cornish ancestry!

CHURCHES IN CORNWALL

There are also brief summaries of Cornish churches in the gazetteer. I have kept these mainly to the parish churches, as to list all the churches in Cornwall of every denomination would run to many pages.

My reasons for including the church details were that I am personally interested in church architecture and, as well as believing these buildings give a unique insight into the history of Cornwall, they certainly beautify their surroundings. My hope is that the more interest and attention they receive the more they are likely to survive.

It can be seen from the abbreviated details given, which churches are the earliest with interesting features. More often than not, Cornish churches have Norman foundations, and most baptismal fonts from that time have survived, so, on the whole, I have not included these in the lists.

The greatest period of church building, whether as a new building, or as an addition to an existing one, was in the fifteenth century. The Reformation in the sixteenth century, meant that the monasteries and abbeys, with their lands and possessions, were taken from the church and many were left to become ruins. Churches were desecrated and statues, icons and stained glass windows destroyed. The building of churches lapsed on the whole, and although there was some revival in the eighteenth century, most buildings soldiered on until they were in such bad condition that drastic work was needed in the nineteenth century. This was when much wonderful medieval work was pulled down, thrown out or burnt and replaced with rather soul-less neo-Gothic interiors.

An example of the general picture in the nineteenth century is at St. Pinnock Church near Liskeard. In the history of the church by B.E. St. Paer-Gotch (holder of a bronze medal given by the Royal Cornwall Polytechnic Society for his history of Jacobstowe church and parish), he writes that "the church is small and plain, pointing to a relatively poor community in the past, with no great lords of the manor who could lavish riches on their church".

By the early 19th century the church was in a sorry state of repair. "In 1822 the whole church is in very bad order, it ought to be entirely new seated and has not been ceiled," he writes. A new rector arrived in 1835 - the first since 1789. He rebuilt the rectory, and lived there until 1870, while the church continued to fall into disrepair.

A report in the Cornish Times of 1882 stated that "no church in the diocese was probably in a worse state than this a year or two ago. The floor was uneven and damp and encumbered with a number of irregular modern deal pews of all shapes and sizes. The original chancel roof had been blown away in a great storm and replaced by some rough timbers and a lath and plaster ceiling. The same storm had displaced the timbers of the nave roof, whilst broken windows and ill-fitting doors admitted the wind and rain from all quarters.

St. Veep Church

"The church has been shamefully served and dreadfully neglected until it has become at last a wretched and almost ruinous building."

The new rector in 1870 called in Hine & Odgers of Plymouth, who estimated the work and their fees would be well over a thousand pounds. In the event the total cost was one thousand five hundred pounds, of which only half came from subscriptions and grants, the rest being met by the rector, who was not particularly wealthy.

Mr. Gotch comments that the church was more fortunate than some as "a genuine attempt seems to have been made to restore rather than Victorianise. As much of the old building as possible was used, old roof timbers re-used and new bosses carved to agree with the old, and quite elegant chancel woodwork, screen and pulpit supplied by Messrs Hems of Exeter. The only unfortunate note is the use of encaustic floor tiles".

Many churches fared badly in their Victorian restoration, but there are still enough beautiful ones with fascinating early details to make them worthy of a visit.

SAINTS AND SINNERS

Saints play a major role in the history of Cornish names, and the places which bear them give distinction to the geography of today's Cornwall, as well as the fascination of colourful legends. These include incredible methods of transport by saints across the seas, and stirring tales of encounters with dragons and other mythical beasts.

Nicholas Orme, a professor of history at Exeter University, reckons there were nearly two hundred Cornish saints, ranging from St. Agnes to St. Zennor. He spent ten years researching them for his book "The Saints of Cornwall", and among his conclusions he states emphatically that St. Piran, who is generally regarded as Cornwall's patron saint of tinners and miners, was Cornish and did not come from Ireland, Wales or Brittany.

St. Piran, or St. Perran, is commemorated in the names of Perranporth, Perranzabuloe, Perranuthnoe, Perran Downs, Perranwell and Perran-ar-worthal.

Cornwall's other great saint is St. Petroc, and here Professor Orme again differs from other experts, such as Catherine Rachel John, whose comprehensive book "The Saints of Cornwall" was published in 1981 with a revised edition in 2001. She says that Petroc, the son of a Welsh king or chieftan, went to Ireland to become a monk and then came by ship to Cornwall, landing in the Camel Estuary. There he founded the monastic centre of Petroc-stow, or Padstowe, where his good deeds included acts of healing, including taking a splinter out of the eye of a dragon. Professor Orme says the saint originated from the Padstow and Bodmin area because it is the centre of a distribution map of his wanderings.

The saints of Cornwall rather belie the image created by the word "saintly". Many lived up to this notion, but others had a more robust way of life, some being murdered by their putative lovers, and others had reactions which were far from the meek and mild character we ascribe to them. St. Minver, for instance, was so incensed by the assault the Devil made on her whilst she was tidying her hair, that she vanquished him by throwing her comb at her tormentor.

One of the most prolific progenitors of saints was the Welsh king Broccan or Brychan. This king from Breconshire in South Wales, was the father of at least 24 children, most of whom founded churches in Cornwall, as well as Devonshire and Wales.

In Cornwall, the places associated with these saints include Advent (St. Adwen), St. Clether, Egloskerry (St.Keri), St. Endellion, Fowey (St. Berry), Gwennap (St. Wynup), St. Issey, St. Juliot (St. Julianna), St. Keyne, Landulph (St. Dilic), St. Mabyn, St. Minver, Morwenstow (St. Morwenna), St. Nectan's Glen, St. Teath and St. Wenn (St. Wenna).

Broccan's eldest son, Nectan, is said to have been buried under the basin into which the water falls at St. Nectan's Glen, near Tintagel, after he had been beheaded by two villains who stole his milk cows.

St. Endelienta, a daughter of King Broccan and god-daughter of King Arthur, was responsible for the siting of the church at St. Endellion, near Padstow, because she was buried where the oxon, who were drawing her burial chariot, stopped and a church subsequently built on the site.

St. Carantoc, of Welsh royal birth, tamed a dragon on his way to Cornwall, where he founded a church at Crantock, near Newquay.

Alley in St. Ives

St. Winwaloe's mother was said to have grown a third breast after giving birth to triplets. As a child, Winwaloe developed healing powers and restored his sister's eye which had been swallowed by a goose.

Another healing saint was St. Blaise, who gave his name to St. Blazey, near St. Austell. He was good at curing throat troubles, giving his blessing with two crossed candles held across the throat. He was also the patron saint of wool combers.

St. Cleer, who founded a church on the southern part of Bodmin Moor, was the victim of more earthly vices. A local noblewoman pursued him, so he fled from her passionate advances into an isolated hermitage, but the lady found him there and had him murdered.

St. Clement, who has many maritime sites dedicated to him including the pretty church near Truro on the Tresillian River, was martyred by being fastened to an anchor and thrown into the sea.

St. Columb ran away from a pagan man who wanted her to marry his son. Because she refused to give up her faith and accede to his wishes, he beheaded her. She is commemorated at a spring near St. Columb Major at Ruthvoes, the name meaning red stones, showing where her blood was shed.

The saints who travelled to Cornwall from Ireland and Wales performed miracles in their method of transport. St. Ia, patron saint of St. Ives, hopped on a leaf; while St. Kea (patron saint of Kea, near Truro) sailed from Ireland in a granite trough.

Of the other saints, the legends include St. Agnes, whom the Romans executed by stabbing her in the throat; St. Budock, who was said to have been born to a Breton princess while she was floating in a barrel after being wrongly accused of betraying her husband; St. Wynerus (patron saint of Gwinear), the son of an Irish king, was martyred in Cornwall with 777 companions by the pagan king Theodoric; St. Newlin (patron saint of Newlyn East), was thought to have been martyred by his father who was a king; St. Sithney is said to be the patron saint of mad dogs, while St. Stephen (patron of St. Stephen in Brannel and other churches) was the first martyr stoned to death in Jerusalem AD 35.

These tales of the saints add colour to the story of Cornwall in its early days, and our admiration for their dedication and life of service.

HOLY WELLS

One of the fascinating aspects of Cornwall is the number of holy wells to be found all over the county - nearly two hundred, many still housed in delightful miniature chapel-like structures.

The definitive guide to these wells was published by Jack Meyrick in 1982. Called "A Pilgrim's Guide to the Holy Wells of Cornwall", the author visited, or re-visited, the wells between 1978 and 1980, travelling in all weathers to remote corners of the Duchy, making notes and taking photographs.

He is to be congratulated on his thorough approach, his persistence in searching out the wells and their sources (even if there was nothing to see except a trickle of water or a few stones), and the engaging historical background he gives for each one.

His widow, Judy Meyrick, told me that her husband was the County Safety Officer with the Ministry of Agriculture and so "knew every farm in Cornwall". It was while chatting to the farmers that he learnt about the holy wells on their land, and when he took early retirement he set himself the task of visiting every one, recording the locations and taking photographs.

Many of the wells associated with the early churches, are usually to be found fairly near them, and named after their patron saints. Others obviously had links with private chapels, and are often in remote locations. The majority of these were difficult to find, so by now they have probably become even more overgrown, or their locations forgotten if the land has changed hands.

The early wells quite often had a resident saint - whether Cornish, Irish, Welsh or Breton. Once a supply of water had been recognised as valuable because of its curative powers and a saint had moved in, then pilgrims, or those searching for a cure, would make their way to the well, stay a night or more, wash in the well once a day at dawn, pray before sunrise after fasting, then drink the water. At the Holy Well of St. Constantine near Harlyn Bay, the well was surrounded by seats, where pilgrims sat after refreshing themselves in the water, and also took part in the ceremonies for bringing on rain after a drought. This well has been preserved by the local Old Cornwall Society.

There are many legends associated with the saints and the wells, but the well today which is probably one of the best known is that at St. Keyne (incidentally pronounced St. Cane, not St. Keen). Here it is said that after the wedding ceremony, the first of the couple to drink at the well will be the one in charge of their subsequent life.

Robert Southey's poem says "If the husband at this gifted well should drink before his wife, a happy man henceforth is he, for he shall be master for life."

And the reply: "I hastened as soon as the wedding was done, and left my wife in the porch. But i'faith she had been wiser than I, for she took a bottle to church."

Competition developed between the parishes - Madron and Bodmin had four wells and Sancreed had two - while a trade in relics developed, many being stolen in pursuit of this commerce.

The custom of tying pieces of rag to a well or nearby branch is said to have arisen from the touching of the garments of St. Audry - hence the word tawdry. The saint for her part thought a tumour in her throat was a punishment for having worn jewelled necklaces.

Jack Meyrick became concerned about the state of many of the wells which he found, and wondered if Old Cornwall Societies or Parish Councils could appoint a volunteer to make an annual inspection and co-ordinate any voluntary work necessary to ensure their preservation.

A member of the Cornwall Archaeological Unit told me their department only has a recording, rather than a custodial, role, but if the well was a scheduled monument it could come under the jurisdiction of the English Heritage Field Warden. If the well was a listed building then it came under the care of the District Council, but the owner of the land on which the well is situated is responsible for its upkeep

CORNISH CROSSES

The most frequently found early monuments in Cornwall are the stone crosses to be seen in the grounds of churches or near them, or sited by roads. There are over 350 - more than in any other county in the British Isles, but this number at one time would have been nearer 400, judging by the bases without crosses which have been found, or have been used for other purposes.

Reasons for erecting so many crosses in Cornwall include guiding the way to church and places where bodies were rested on the way to burial. Many in trackless wastes were put up as guides or markers, especially at road intersections, and the custom was for wealthy pilgrims to leave alms at the crosses for the poorer folk who followed them.

Arthur Langdon in his large, well-researched and illustrated book of 1896 reckoned that none of the Christian monuments in Cornwall are older than the 5th century, and those showing Saxon influences are probably of the 10th and 11th centuries.

The Celtic patterns on the Cornish crosses, he says, are more akin to those in Wales than in Ireland, Scotland or Northumbria. The Cornish crosses tend to have plain stylised crosses or the figure of Christ, not many having interlaced work or other ornament.

T.F.G. Dexter and Henry Dexter in their book "Cornish Crosses: Christian and Pagan", point out that many stones were originally pagan, worked with Sun or Fertility Symbols. The cross so frequently seen, they say, was originally a Greek cross or wheel, which is a Sun symbol.

Whoever is right on this point, it is good to see that so many crosses are being rescued and re-sited - the cross in front of Truro Cathedral being a good example.

Cornish Cross at Trenethick Barton
Helston

Many changes have of course come about since Arthur Langdon produced his book, so excellently illustrated with the designs on the crosses clearly shown. Those wanting to follow in his footsteps, however, may be very disappointed. Many crosses have been moved, often to save them - the gentry at that time, for instance, often moved crosses into their gardens in the cause of preservation, but this meant that the crosses lost their original setting and purpose - even if they made wonderful ornaments!

The designs on the crosses have also become eroded through wind and weather, and are not always easy to find. However, I would be grateful if readers would let me know if the locations I have given for crosses in the listing in their area are now incorrect.

Note: All location measurements are in miles, taken from the centre of the nearest town or place. Distances are approximate and as the crow flies. Church Descriptions give basic dates and outstanding features, but not usually Norman fonts as most churches possess one.

Cornish Crosses: Details of crosses given below have been based on those in Arthur Langdon's book of 1896 (reprinted in 1988). Many of these crosses have subsequently been moved or disintegrated. Any new information about these would be welcome.

Meanings: Many of the meanings of place names are very obscure and the right origins are a matter for debate. In many cases the alternatives have been given, even though they appear to be very different.

Pronunciation: I have used my own phonetic method of pronunciation, with the parts of words to be emphasised written in capital letters.

Place	Pronunciation	Location	Meaning

A

Acton Castle	ACT'un Castle	2.5m SE Marazion off A394	

Detail: Castellated mansion, 1775 for Admiral Stackhouse

Advent	AD'vnt	1m SE Camelford off A39	From St. Adwena.

Details:The saint is said to be one of 24 children of King Broccan and Queen Gladwison of Breconshire. Sometimes referred to as St.Anne or St.Tane, she is said to be the patron saint of sweethearts. Church,stands alone,has tower of eight pinnacles (probably only one in Cornwall, says Pevsner), 13C 15C, restored 1848,has wagon roofs, flamboyant E window, carved bosses in aisles & porch.Cornish cross W of church.

Aire Point	Air Point	2m NE Land's End off A30	Rock on a height

Detail: From old Cornish word aro (height)

Albaston	Al'VAS'tun	1m SW Gunnislake off A390	Alva's farm (from Old English 'Alvas tun')
Allen River	AL'n River	From N. Cornwall runs into River Camel at Sladesbridge.	

Detail: Name changed three times - Dewi, Laine, and Allen in late 19C, which could mean 'white' or 'shining'.

Allet	AL'it	3m NW Truro off A30	Probably Celtic river name meaning 'nourisher'
Alsia	ALE'yer	1m SW St. Buryan off B3283	Sloping land.

Detail: Holy well on Lower Alsia Farm where sick children were bathed in its waters.

Altarnun	OL'ta'NUN	8m SW Launceston off A30	Altar of St. Nonn

Details: The saint was the mother of St. David. Church, 15C 16C, restored 1867,has tall tower, wagon roofs,rood screen, 79 bench ends,altar rail 1684, grand Norman font, slate memorial by Neville Northey Burnard, born in village, tomb of Isbells 1795. Cornish cross in churchyard, cross head in vicarage garden.Holy well of St. Nonna .25m NE renowned for cure of madmen.

Alverton	AL'vr'tun	in W Penzance	Alward's place.

Detail: Lords of the Manor of Alverton fostered growth of Penzance

Amalveor	AM'ul'veer	2.5m SW St. Ives off B3306	Great slope
Anderton	AND'er'tun	2m S Torpoint off B3247	Lower farm or The oak on the meadow

14

Methodist Chapel, Altarnun with head of Wesley by local sculptor Neville Northey Burnard

Andrewartha	**An'droo'WARTH'a**	NE Penryn off A39	Upper farm
Angarrack	**An'GA'rick**	2m E Hayle off A30	The rock

Detail: Granite viaduct of 1885

Angarrick	**An'GA'rick**	2m NE Penryn off A39	The rock
Antron	**AN'trun**	1.5m SW Penryn off A394 or B3291	The nose
Antony	**AN'tun'ni**	2.5m W Torpoint off A374	Anta's farm

Details: Early 18C National Trust house and gardens. Church in village, dedicated to St. James, 13C 15C, has piscinas, sedilia, pulpit 1500, "most spectacular early brass in Cornwall of Margery Arundell" (Pevsner) & Carew memorials. Maryfield Church (once an estate church for the house) built 1865 by William White.

Argal	**AR'gl**	1.5m SW Penryn off A394	Retreat

Detail: Water park and fishing

Arwenack	**AR'WEN'ick**	in E Falmouth (near docks) off A39	Facing a marshy place

Detail: Earliest house in Falmouth, built by Killigrews

Ashton	**ASH'tun**	3.5m W Helston on A394	Ash tree village

Detail: Founded 1867

Atlantic Highway	**AtLANtic Highway**	A39 road from Bude to Newquay	

Details: New name, given in November 2002, named after the Southern Railway's Atlantic Coast Express which ran daily from Waterloo between 1926 and 1966.

Avarack	**Av'rack**	2m NE St. Just on B3306	Arable land
Ayr	**Air**	in W St. Ives	High place

B

| Baldhu | Bal'DEW | 3m SW Truro between A39 & A390 | Black mine. |

Details: Church of 1848 by William White from design by Rev William Haslam, curate of the parish. Memorial to Cornish preacher Billy Bray. Church now closed. Holy well in churchyard.

| Balleswidden | Bals'WID'n | in St. Just on A3071 | Mine near farm at Leswidden (white ruins) from china clay deposits. |

| Ballowall Barrow | B'LOW'el (as in 'cow') Barrow | .5m W St. Just off B3306 | Louhal's dwelling. |

Detail: Chambered cairn. National Trust/English Heritage

Balwest	Bal'west	1m NW Ashton off A394	West mine
Barbican	BARB'i'cun (old name Porthbyhen)	in E Looe off A387	Little cove (old name for West Looe)
Barcelona	Bar'c'lona	2m W Looe off B3359	Called Trelawne Cross in 1637, but re-named Barcelona in 18C, possibly by a Trelawn.
Bareppa	B'REP'er	1m N Mawnan Smith	Beautiful retreat (from Fr. - beau repaire)
Barkla Shop	Bark'la Shop	1m E St. Agnes on B3285	Barkla's workshop or forge
Barncoose	Barn'COOZ	.5m W Redruth on A3047	Wood top
Barnoon	Bar'noon	in central St. Ives	Top of the down
Barripper	B'RIP'er	1.5m SW Camborne off B3303	Beautiful retreat (from Fr. - beau repaire)
Barteliver	Bar't'LEEver	.5m SW Grampound off A390	Nook
Bartinney Downs	Bar'TIN'ee Downs	2m SE St. Just off A3071	Prominent hill fort
Bathpool	Barth'pool	7m SW Launceston off B3254	Pool in River Lynher
Beacon	Bee'kun	Southern edge of Camborne off B3303	Hill
Bedruthan Steps	B'DRUTH'in Steps ('uth' as in 'dove')	5m N Newquay off B3276	Ruthin's farm.

Details: Information Centre & teashop in Count House office of former Carnewas Iron Mine. National Trust

Belowda	B'LOWD'a	1.5m NW Victoria .5m off A30	Louda's dwelling (known as Belowzy in 1602 and Belovely in 1870)
Benellack	Ben'AL'eck	1m NW Grampound off A390	Broom brake
Berepper	B'REP'er	3m S Helston off A3083, near Gunwalloe	Beautiful retreat (from Fr. - beau repaire)
Berriowbridge	BERRY'o'bridge	6m SW Launceston off B3254	Kites' bridge

Detail: Medieval bridge of three arches.

| Bessy Benath | Bessy B'NATH | nr Veryan off A3078 | Bessy's dwelling (has been translated as Bessy Beneath, said to be where a witch is buried). |
| Bethel | Beth'l | NE edge St. Austell on A391 | Hall meadow |

16

Bin Down	BIN'down	2.5m NE Looe between A387 & B3253	Binna's hill
Biscovey	Bis'co 'VAY	3.5m E St. Austell off A390	Kenevy's dwelling

Detail: Mid-Cornwall Galleries

| Bishop Rock | Bishop Rock | 6m W St. Agnes, Isles of Scilly | Probably from its shape. |

Detail: In 1302, convicted thieves, Muriel de Trenywith and two daughters, were left there to be drowned. Lighthouse, furthest West, built 1887.

Bissoe	BISS'o	4m SW Truro off A39	Birch trees
Blackwater	BLACK'water	3m E Redruth off A30	Black stream

Detail: John Passmore Edwards, philanthropist, born here.

| Blisland | BLIZ'lund | 4.5m NE Bodmin off A30 | Bloia's farm |

Details: Village green with interesting houses. Church dedicated to St. Protus and St. Hyacinth, who were Roman martyrs, has all styles from Norman onwards, restored 1896, has two fonts, wagon roofs, rood screen, Jacobean pulpit, restored 1912, Royal Arms 1604, brass 1410, slate 1624. Early manor house on the NE corner of the green. Trippet Stones on common 1m NE has circle of 8 standing and 12 fallen stones. Holy well of St. Pratts .25m E of church. Tregenna Holy Well .5m N.

Blowinghouse	Blowinghouse (or Blowing'ouse)	2m NE St. Agnes off B3284	Smelting house or old tin foundry
Blowing House Hill	Blowing'ouse Hill	W of Redruth on A3047	Smelting house or old tin foundry on hill
Blunts	Blunts	6m NW Saltash, 2m off A38	Named after local family ?
Bochym	B'CHIM	5m SE Helston off A3083	Goat's fold

Details: In 14C & 15C was residence of Le Bret family. Additions to building made in later centuries.

| Boconnoc | B'CON'uck | 3m E Lostwithiel off A390 | Connoc's dwelling. |

Details: Thomas Pitt, grandfather of William Pitt, England's youngest prime minister,bought estate in 1717 and landscaped 8,000 acres to include deer park and lake. House,1719 & later,and park open to public occasionally. Church nr house, 15C, restored 1873, has Jacobean altar, pulpit 1629,rood screen,old timber in roof etc,musicians' gallery. Cornish cross in churchyard and two in park.

| Bodelva | Bd'EL'va | 1m NW St. Blazey Gate off A390 | Elm trees place |

Detail: Eden Project.

Bodieve	B'DEEVE	.5m N of Wadebridge just off A39	Lord's dwelling
Bodilly	B'DILL'i	2.5m NE Helston off B3297	Deli's or Ili's dwelling
Bodinnick	B'DIN'ik	opposite Fowey across river	Dwelling by a fort.

Detail: St. John's - small church built in stable by parishioners 1948. Hall Farm has remains of chapel with bell turret and Norman doorway. Daphne du Maurier lived at Ferryside.

| Bodmin | BOD'min | off A30 | Monks' dwelling |

Details: Largest parish church in Cornwall, dedicated to St. Petroc with unique early reliquary;separate 14C chantry chapel;remains of priory;seven holy wells. Cornish crosses outside jail and Berry Tower.Shire Hall & Town Museum; Jail; St. Lawrence's Hospital (converted); Military Museum; Steam railway. Famous sons: Sir Arthur Quiller Couch and John Arnold, 18C clocks & maritime chronometer maker.Bodmin Riding July. Tourist office: Shire Hall, Mount Folly Sq. 01208-76616

Daphne du Maurier's house at Bodinnick, near Fowey.

This was the house at Bodinnick, called Ferryside, which the famous author first saw at the age of 19. The locals called it Swiss Cottage. Boats were built there with lofts on the second floor and living space at the top. Writing in her book "Vanishing Cornwall" of her initial view of the house, she compared it to a lover looking for the first time on a chosen one. "I for this, and this for me". She bought the property and spent many happy hours there writing, sailing, walking and dreaming, and was eventually married from it, leaving for the church by boat.

Name	Pronunciation	Location	Meaning
Bodmin Moor	BOD'min More	Area of moorland bounded by Bodmin, Liskeard, Launceston and Camelford	

Detail: Originally called Foy Moor (Moorland of the River Fowey)

Name	Pronunciation	Location	Meaning
Bodrifty	Bur'DRIFT'i	2m NW Madron	Dwelling by hedge

Detail: Iron Age settlement.

Name	Pronunciation	Location	Meaning
Bodwen	B'dWEN	6m N St. Austell off A391	Wenn's house or White dwelling
Bohortha	Bo'hurra	1m SE St. Mawes by ferry off A3078	Cow yards
Bojewyan	Bo'JEW'un	2.5m NW St. Just on B3306	Uyon's farm or Little cowhouse
Bolenowe	B'LEN'a	3m SW Redruth off B3280	Dwelling by land strip farm or pools

Detail: Vincent's Holy well to E.

Name	Pronunciation	Location	Meaning
Bolingey	B'LINJ'ee	.5m SE Perranporth off B3284	Millhouse
Bolster	Boll'ster	.5m SW St. Agnes off B3277 near Bolster Farm	Boat-like hump

Detail: Earthwork resembling an upturned boat nearby. Name also given to the giant said to have built the earthwork.

Name	Pronunciation	Location	Meaning
Bolventor	Bol'VENT'er	10m NE Bodmin just off A30	Bold venture (farming village in middle of moor)

Detail: Church of Holy Trinity, built 1848, nr site of medieval chapel of St. Luke.

Name	Pronunciation	Location	Meaning
Booby's Castle	BOO'Bees Castle	2.5m SW St. Ives on B3311 near Cripplesease	Named after owner ?
Bonython	B'NIGH'thun	4.5m SE Helston off A3083	Dwelling in the furze

Detail: 18C house with earlier foundations ,named after original owners. Gardens open to public

Name	Pronunciation	Location	Meaning
Bosahan	Bs'ANN	.5m N Constantine in between Falmouth & Helston	John's house, or Dwelling in dry place
Bosahan	Bs'AYN	1m NW Manaccan, S side of Helford River	John's house or Dwelling in dry place
Bosavern	Boz'AV'ern	.5m S St. Just off B3306	Avarn or Awern's dwelling
Boscadjack	Bs'CADJ'ick	2m NE Helston off B3297	Dwelling with daisies
Boscastle	BOS'castle	4m N Camelford on the B3266	Boterel's castle

Details: From castle in N village of major Norman family Botreaux. Harbour. Museum of Witchcraft. Old Forge Visitor Centre 01840-250010.

Name	Pronunciation	Location	Meaning
Boscaswell (Higher & Lower)	B'SKAWL	2m NE St. Just off B3306	Caswal's dwelling

Detail: Holy well on w edge of Lower Boscaswell

Name	Pronunciation	Location	Meaning
Boscawen-noon	Bs'CO'en Noon (or B'Scaw'NOON)	1.5m NE St. Buryan off A30	Dwelling by elder tree on the down
Boscawen-Un	Bs'CO'en Oon (or B'Scaw'OON)	1m N St. Buryan off A30	Dwelling by elder tree on the down

Detail: Bronze Age circle of 19 stones

Name	Pronunciation	Location	Meaning
Boscawen Rose	Bs'CO'en Ros (or B'Scaw' ROS)	2m SE St. Buryan off B3315	Dwelling by elder tree on moorland

Boscoppa	Boz'COP'a	NE fringe of St. Austell	Coppa's dwelling
Boscundle	Bz'CUN'dl	1m E St. Austell off A390	Cundle's dwelling?
Boscreege	Bs'CREEG	1.5m NW Ashton off A394	Dwelling by an ancient barrow
Boskenna Cross	Bz'KENNA Cross	1.5m SE St. Buryan on B3315	Kenow's dwelling or Dwelling on hill ridge

Detail: Cornish Cross found in hedge 1896, mounted in middle of three crossroads on granite from cider mill, hit frequently by traffic, re-sited and restored by English Heritage in 2002. Boskenna Nurseries to SW.

Boskennal	Bs'KEN'l	.5m SE St. Buryan off B3283	Cenwal's dwelling
Boslowick	Bz'LO'ick	Southern fringe of Falmouth	Copse by a pool at Little Prislow (formerly Preslowyk)
Bosporthennis	Bs'PREN'iss	2m SW Zennor off B3306	Dwelling at entrance to isolated spot
Bossiney	B'SIN'ee	.5m NE Tintagel off B3263	Cyni's or Kyni's dwelling

Detail: Sir Francis Drake MP in 1584. Author J.B. Priestley lived in Old Borough House

Busullow	Bs'ULL'o	4m NE St. Just off B3306	Dwelling by a cottage of light
Bosvigo	Boz'VI'go	W fringe of Truro off A390	Wiga's dwelling

Detail: Gardens and nurseries with unusual plants

Boswinger	Boz'wen'jer	1m W Gorran Haven on B3273	Gwengor's dwelling
Botallack	B'TAL'ek	1m N St. Just on B3306	Tallock's dwelling or Dwelling on a steep hill.

Detail: 19C mines. National Trust.

Botus Fleming	Boz'flem'en	2.5m NW Saltash off A388	Dwelling of Flumiet (corrupted to Fleming)?

Details: Church of St. Mary, 15C, restored 1872, has good N arcade with carving and niches, piscina, tablet to Michael Loam, inventor of miners' man-engine. Obelisk to William Martyn outside churchyard. St. Mary's Holy well E of church, stone building with statue of Virgin Mary inside

Bowithick	B'with'ick?	.5m N Altarnun off A30	Dwelling in treed place

Detail: 17C packhorse bridge

Boyton	BOY'tun	5m N Launceston off B3254	Boya's or Boia's farm

Details: Church, dedicated to The Holy Name, 14C, 15C, restored 1877, has early font, piscina, rood screen base, wagon roofs, tablet 1662 to benefactor.

Bradford	Bradford	2m NE Blisland off A30	Broad ford (from Old English)

Detail: Clapper bridges. Wilderness sculpture garden.

Braddock	BRAD'uck	4m NE Lostwithiel off A390	Broad oak or Broad hook of land (from Old English)

Detail: Church of St.Mary, 15C, restored 19C, has wagon roofs, Elizabethan pulpit, rood screen base, carved pew fronts, alabaster reredos. St.Mary's well to NW.

Brane	Brain	1.5m N St. Buryan off A30	Crow's or Bran's dwelling

Details: Bran is the name of a Welsh mythological figure associated with hill forts. The hillfort nearby is called Caer Bran (crow's fort or fort near Brane). Megalithic tomb.

Bosvigo House, Truro

Bray Shop	**BRAY Shop**	3.5m NW Callington on B3257	Bray's workshop
Brea	**Bray**	1m E Camborne off A3047	Hill
Breage	**Breeg** or **Brayg (older)**	3m W Helston on A394	From St. Breaca.

Details: The saint was one of group of missionaries from Ireland who landed at Hayle. Church, 15C, restored 1891, has large 15C wall paintings, Roman milestone. Cornish sandstone cross, only one of its kind in Cornwall - legend says it is made of blood and sand from a battle fought at foot of Godolphin Hill.

Bridge	**Bridge**	2.5m NW Redruth on B3300	Bridge over river
Brighton	**BRY'tun**	7.5m NW St. Austell on A3058	Bright farm

Detail: Thought might have been named in 1888 after Brighton in Sussex, which was Beorhthelm's farm.

Brightor	**BRI'ter**	4m NW Saltsh off A38	Bright hill or Variegated land
Brill	**Brill**	5m SW Falmouth off A394	Hunt hill
Brisons	**BRISS'uns**	1m SW off Cape Cornwall	From Fr."brisant" reef or shoal of rocks
Brown Gelly	**Brown Gelly** (hard G)	2.5m S Jamaica Inn off A30, nr Colliford Lake	Grove hill

Brown Willy	Brown WILL'y	2.5m NW Jamaica Inn at Bolventor off A30	Hill of swallows or Highest hill
Bryher	Bray'yer	3.5m NW St. Mary's, Isles of Scilly	Place of hills.

Details: All Saints church built 1742, rebuilt and enlarged 1822. Chambered tomb on Samson Hill, and round barrows on Shipman Head Down.

Bude	Bewd	on A39	Probably after muddy stream called Bedewater - or after family named Beede

Details: Surfing Centre, 1823 Canal, Museum, Bude Millennium Light(30ft) to commemorate Sir Goldsworthy Gurney,who lit House of Commons in 1850's. His house, The Castle,built 1835, now Town Council offices. Church of St. Michael and All Angels 1835 by Wightwick, with later additions. Vicarage said to have been manor of Sir John Arundel in 15C. Ebbingford Manor, early building restored 1758. Display at Helebridge on canal. Tourist Office: The Crescent 01288- 354240.

Buckshead	BUCKS'head	Northern fringe of Truro on A39	Buck's hill
Budock Water	BEW'dock Water	.5m w Falmouth S of A39	From St. Budoc

Details: The saint is said to have been born to a Breton princess whilst she was floating in a barrel. Church, 13-15C, has piscinas, low box pews, rood screen with painted panels,brass Sir John Killigrew 1567. Two wheel crosses in churchyard.

Bugle	Bew'gl	4m N St. Austell on A391	Probably named after

coaching stop called Bugle Inn, around which village grew (inn built 1840), the name commemorating the prowess of a local player or the coaching guard.

Burlawn	B'LAWN	1.5m S Wadebridge off A39	Happy dwelling or Lowen's dwelling
Burncoose	Burn'COOZ	3m SE Redruth off A393	Wooded area on breast of hill.

Detail: Nurseries. Garden open to public

Burnewhall	Ber'NEW'ull	1.5m S St. Buryan off B3315	Dwelling in the mist.

Details: Estate owned 14C by Robertus de Burnewhall; in 17C by William Noye, Attorney General to Charles II, said to have hidden there on his flight to France.

Burngullow	Burn'GULL'o	2.5m W St. Austell off A3058	Bright hill
Burras	B'russ	5m SW Redruth on B3297	Short ford
Burraton	Ber'tun	3.5m SE Callington off A388	Farm by fort
Buryas Bridge	Ber'i 'as Bridge	1.5m SW Penzance on A30	Berry's bridge

Detail: Bridge built 1774. Trewidden gardens, noted for camellias.

Bussow	Bosow	1.5m SW St. Ives off B3311	Dwellings

Detail: Hut circles, medieval dovecote

Busvannah	Bus'VARNah	1m NE Penryn off A39	Monks' dwelling
Buttern Hill	But'n Hill?	3m NW Altarnun off A30	Meadow hill

Detail: Bronze Age stone

C

Cadgwith   KAJ'with   2m NE Lizard off A3083   Thicket bush harbour

Cadson Bury   CAD'sun'berry   2m SW Callington   Fort by Cadda's farm.
off A390

Detail: Iron Age Fort. National Trust.

Caerhays   Kar'HAYS   8m SW St. Austell   Enclosed fort?
off B3287

Details: May be linked with Carhaix in Finisterre. Castle house by John Nash built 1808.Gardens open to public.

Calamansack   Calla'MAN'seck   5m SW Falmouth   Retreat on small hill
or K'MAN'sek

Calenick   Cal'IN'ick   .75m S Truro off A39   Holly grove

Callestick   Cal'ES'tick   3.5m E St. Agnes   Obscure
off A3075

Detail: Holy? well S of village. Cider Farm

Callington   CAL'ing'tun   on A390 between   Bare hill settlement
Liskeard & Tavistock   (Kit Hill is nearby).

Detail: Church, dedicated to St. Mary, consecrated 1438, restored 1858, has unusual clerestory, wagon roofs, piscina, brass 1466 to benefactor Nicholas Aysshton, alabaster monument to Sir Robert Willoughby de Broke 1502. Lantern cross in churchyard. Old clink. Annual Honey Fair. Castlewich Henge lm SE.

Calstock   CAL'stock   4.5m E Callington   Outlying farm.
off A390 on River Tamar

Detail: Church, dedicated to St. Andrew,13-15C,restored 1887,has Edgcumbe Chapel 1588 with 17C monuments,damaged wall painting of St. George and the Dragon, stoup. Rectory 1853 by Decimus Burton. Twelve-arched railway viaduct across Tamar. Holy well of St. Andrew once in Rectory glebe (no remains).

Calvadnack   Cul'VAD'nack   4m SW Redruth   Place of sparrows in
off B3297   prominent position

Detail: Ancient settlement

Camborne   CAM'bern   3.5m SW Redruth   Crooked hill
or CAM'born   on A3047

Detail: Home of Richard Trevithick, pioneer of steam engine which fired Industrial Revolution. Built first steam-powered "road-car" which ran up Camborne Hill on Christmas Eve 1801. Centre of mining and Methodism, Museum, statue of Trevithick, Literary Inst.1829. Parish church,dedicated first to St. Meriadoc,a companion of Gwinear, and from 15C also to St. Martin, is 15C, restored 1774, 1862, 1878, has piscina, altar slab of 10C, reredos 1761, pulpit 1480 and 18C, 19C monuments. Cornish Cross and base in churchyard, another near Institute. Holy well of St. Meriasek .25m N of church. Trevithick Day, April.

Camel Rock   Camel Rock   nr Porthleven on the S. West Coastal Footpath
From the resemblance to head of a camel formed from rocks (also known as The Bishop).

Camel River   Camel River   upper reaches wind down from Camelford, by St. Breward, to Wadebridge, emerging at Padstow. Crooked or curved suggested (former name of main river was Alan)

Camelford   CAMML'fud   on A39 bet. Launceston   Ford of River Camel.
& Wadebridge

Detail: Modern church of St. Thomas (1938) by Sir Charles Nicholson.Town Hall 1806. North Cornwall Museum and Art Gallery, Indian King Arts Centre. British Cycling Museum. Tourist Office: The Clease 01840-212954. Camel Trail - 16 mile footpath & cycleway along old rail track between Padstow and Blisland.

Camel weathervane
at Camelford

Canon's Town	CANONS'town	2.5m SW Hayle off A30	Named after Exeter Cathedral Canon, John Rogers of Penrose, Helston (1778-1856).
Canworthy Water	CAN'worthy Water	8m E Boscastle off A39 below Canworthy farm	Hamlet by River Ottery
Cape Cornwall	Cape CORN'wul	1.5m NW St. Just off A3071	English name, Cape Cornwall, from 1690.

Details: Was originally Kil Gooth East (goose -back at St. Just) from its shape. Said to be the most westerly point in Cornwall. National Trust. Remains of medieval St. Helen's Chapel.

| Caradon Hill | CARA'dun Hill | 4m NE Liskeard off B3254 | Hill at Carn |

Detail: Named from nearby Caradon Town, which has Holy well of St. John the Baptist on village green.

| Carbis Bay | CAR'bis Bay | 1.5m SE St. Ives off A3074 | 19C village named from bay, which in turn was named from farm at Carbis, meaning cart-bridge or causeway. Bay was originally Porthreptor. |

Detail: Church dedicated to St. Anta (who also gave her name to Lelant) built 1927-68, architect R.F. Wheatly of Truro, has stone from old mine buildings, granite altar, stained glass with Cornish themes, ring of ten bells (only other at Cathedral).

| Carclaze | Car'CLAZE | Northern fringe of St. Austell off A391 | Grey/green ancient barrow |

Carclew	Car'CLOO	2.5m N Penryn off A39	Coloured barrow or tumulus (although none found)

Detail: Mansion of 1740 and 1749 gutted by fire 1934.

Cardinham	Car'DIN'um	4m NE Bodmin off A30	Hill fort

Detail: By coincidence the Dynham family owned the manor in 13C. Patron St.Meubred,a hermit said to be the son of an Irish King,has window to him in St. Neot church. Church, mainly 15C, was damaged in WW2, has sedilia, sepulchral niche, wagon roofs, bench ends,seats, Royal Arms 1661,stocks. Several Celtic crosses in parish, one near church, dated 800AD, is one of the finest in Britain. Inscribed stones 6C or 7C nr church. In area are Holy well of Bellarmin on St. Bellarmin's Tor,with chapel foundations, and Holy well of Trezance. Earthwork castle built by Richard Fitz - Turold, first lord of Cardinham,in late 11C. He is said to have given a traditional grey cloak to the agent of the Earl of Cornwall once a year at Polson Bridge. Another legend says that a woman losing her chastity should do penance on a black sheep.

Cargenwen	Car'GEN'wen	3m S Camborne off B3280	Kenwyn's fort or Fort on white ridge

Detail: Large reservoir

Cargreen	CAR'green?	2.5m NE Saltash off A388	Seal rock
Carharrack	Car-HA'rick (HA as in apple)	2m E Redruth on B3298	High fort

Detail: Gwennap Pit, Methodist preaching pit nearby.

Carkeel	Car'KEEL	1.5m NW Saltash off A388	Ridge fort
Carland Cross	KAR'land Cross	6m NE Truro off A30 (main roundabout)	Sheep or animal fold (from nearby Cowland farm)
Carleen	Car'LEEN	3m NW Helston off B3302	Slate fort
Carlidnack	Car'LID'nick	N fringe of Mawnan Smith	Carlinick's hill fort or Holly grove
Carloggas	Kar'LOG'us	4m NE Newquay off A3059	Hill fort of mice
Carlyon Bay	Kar'LI'on Bay	2m W St. Austell off A3082	Flat stone fort

Detail: Named after Carlyon family, local estate owners

Carminowe Cross	Car'MIN'o Cross	1.5m SE Bodmin at roundabout on A30	Little rock.

Detail: Iron Age fort

Carnanton	Car'NUN'tun	4m NE Newquay off A3059	Rock pile farm

Detail: Nuns Well in woods near Nanskeval.

Carn Brea	Carn'BRAY	1m SW Redruth off A3047	Rocky outcrop above village.

Details: Ancient hill fort, castle, Basset monument 1836. Restaurant.

Carn Euny	Carn YOU'nee	2m N St. Buryan off A30	St. Uny's tor

Details: Chapel site.Holy wells. English Heritage.

Carne	Carn	5m NE St. Mawes off A3078	Rock pile or Bronze Age barrow (Carne Beacon).

Detail: King Gerent, 8C King of Cornwall, believed buried in boat here.

Carne	Carn	2.5m NW St. Keverne off B3293	Rock pile or Bronze Age by Gillan Creek barrow

Carnewas	Carn'NEW'us	5m N Newquay off B3276	Tor by summer pasture.

Detail: National Trust information centre and tea garden over-looking Bedruthan Steps

Carn Galva	Carn GOL'va	2.5m SW Zennor off B3306	Look out tor.

Detail: Engine houses. National Trust.

Carn Gloose	Carn GLOOz	1m W St. Just off A3071	Grey rock
Carnhell Green	CARN'il Green	2.5m SW Camborne off B3303	Tor near a grassy plot at Carnhell

Detail: Carnhell farm 1249, hamlet founded late 18C or early 19C.

Carn Kenidjack	**Carn K'NID'jick**	1m NW St. Just	Hooting tor (from wind sound)
Carnkie	**Carn'KY**	1.5m SW Redruth off B3297	Dog's tor

Detail: Copper mine buildings, closed 1918

Carn Marth	**Carn'MARTH**	1m SE Redruth off A393	Horse tor or Mark's tor.

Detail: Figgy Dowdy's, or Margery Daw's Well near Rocky Field

Carnmenellis	**Carn'mn'ELL'is**	4m S Redruth off B3297	Tor with rocks stacked like sheaves.

Detail: Church of Holy Trinity 1849 with Norman font. Cornish cross in churchyard.

Carnon Downs	**Car'nun DOWNS**	3m SW Truro off A39	Rocky place.

Detail: 19/20C village built on moorland belonging to a group of farms called Carnon

Carnsew	**Carn'SOO**	1m W Penryn off A394	Black rock
Carnyorth	**Carn'YORTH**	1m N St. Just on B3306	Roebuck crag
Caroe	**Ki'ro**	4.5m E Boscastle off A39	Stag fort
Carrick Roads	**Ca'rick Roads**	Estuary from Falmouth	Anchorage of the rock to Feock
Carrine	**K'REEN**	2m SW Truro off A390	Cold fort
Carthew	**Car'THEW**	2.5m N St. Austell on B3274	Black fort

Detail: Wheal Martyn China Clay Centre

Carvallack	**K'VALL'uk**	5m SE Helston off B3293	Maeloc's fort
Carvossa	**K'VOSS'a**	7m NE Truro off A390	Fort with ditches
Carwinion	**Car'WIN'un**	.5m SE Mawnan Smith	White tor or Pleasant dwelling

Detail: Bamboo garden, open to public. Anthony Rogers/ National Trust.

Carwynnen	Car'WIN'un	2m S Camborne off B3303	White tor
Castilly	Cas'TILL'ee	3.5m SW Bodmin off A391	Castles

Detail: Neolithic henge remodelled as medieval amphitheatre

Castle-an-Dinas	Car'sl-an-DYE'nus or Castle Dennis	2.5m SE St. Columb Major off A30.	Iron Age castle hill fort near farm called Dennis.

Detail: Cador, Duke of Cornwall, said to have been killed here. Cornwall Heritage Trust.

Castle-an-Dinas	Car'sl-an-DYE-nus	3.5m SW St. Ives off B3311	Hill fort

Detail: Iron Age hill fort with sham gothic castle, built 1798, called Roger's Tower.

Castle Canyke	Car'sl KAN'ik	1.5m SE Bodmin off A38	Castle on small ridge
Castle Dore	Car'sl DOOR	2m NW Fowey on B3269	Earth work castle

Detail: Site associated with Tristan & Isolde

Castle Horneck	Car'sl HAW'nick	W fringe of Penzance off A30	Iron bearing ground near hill fort (possibly from nearby fort of Lesingey Round).

Detail: Borlase family mansion built 1720, now a Youth Hostel. Holy well of Castle Horneck to SE.

Castlewich	Car'sl'wik	1m SE Callington off A388	Castle by wooded settlement

Detail: Circular henge

Catchall	Catch'ull	3m SW Penzance off A30	From French "chasse" (hunting) to catch
Catchfrench	CATCH'french	5m SE Liskeard off A38	From French "chasse franche" (free hunting or unenclosed hunting land)

Detail: House & garden remodelled by Humphrey Repton.

Cawsand	COR'sand	3m S Torpoint off B3247	Cow's sand

Details: Until the mid 19C the border with Devon passed between Cawsand and Kingsand at the stream next to the Devon Corn building. Old smuggling centre. Best Kept Village in Cornwall in 2001.

Chacewater	CHACE'water	4.5m W Truro off A390	Stream on hunting land

Details: The chace belonged to the Manor of Blanchland or Gooden, first mentioned in the Tristan legend. St. Paul's church built 1828, repaired 1886,damaged by lightning and rebuilt 1892 by Edmund Sedding, has wagon roof, stained glass from St. Mary, Truro. Roseland House garden and nursery. Mines to west.

Chapel Amble	Chapel AM'bull	2m N Wadebridge off A391	Part of Amble with a chapel (the others being Middle and Lower Amble)

Detail: Patron St. Aldhem, the first bishop of Sherborne. Cornwall was in his diocese,and when he visited he addressed a letter to King Gerent pointing out the date on which Easter should be kept.

Chapel Carn Brea	Chapel Carn Bray	2m SE St. Just off B3306	Chapel of the cairn hill.

Detail: Chapel was originally on Neolithic cairn on the hill. National Trust.

Chapel Point	Chapel Point	1.5m SE Mevagissey	Chapel land or point

Details: Chapel mentioned 1327, but no remains found. Nearby is the 50ft cliff from which Sir Henry Bodrugan leapt to escape his pursuer Sir Richard Edgcumbe. National Trust. Interesting houses 1934-39 by J.A. Campbell.

Chapel Porth	Chapel PORTH	1.5m SW St. Agnes off B3277	Chapel cove, named from the former hilltop chapel of St. Agnes

Charlestown	CHARLZ'town	1m SE St. Austell off A390	Charles' town

Details: Harbour was originally Porthmeor (or Great Cove), but name changed after Charles Rashleigh developed port in 18C. St. Paul's church by Eales 1849 with fibreglass spire 1972.Shipwreck & Heritage Centre. Also location of Square Sail Ships and setting for films and television productions.

Cheesewring	Chees'ring	5m N Liskeard off B3254	Monument of stones looking like a cider press - the cheese being the apple mulch.

Detail: Daniel Gumb's cave nearby where 18C eccentric brought up large family.

Chilsworthy	CHILS'worthy	3.5m NE Callington off A390	Ceol's farm.
Chun Castle	Choon Castle	3m NE St. Just off B3306	House on downland.

Detail: Stone built early hillfort, Chun Quoit nearby has four uprights supporting massive capstone.

Chyandour	Shy'an'DOWER	NE fringe of Penzance off A30	House by the water
Chybucca	Shy'BUCK'a	3.5m NW Truro on B3284	Sprite or goblin's house
Chynhalls Point	Shy'nawls Point	2.5m S St. Keverne off B3294	Cliff house
Chysauster	Shy'SAW'ster	3m N Penzance off B3311	Sylvester's house. From farm of Chisalvestre (1313)

Detail: Ancient village of well-preserved courtyard houses. English Heritage.

Chyvelah	Shy-VEE-la	2m W Truro	Highest house
Chyverton	CHIV'r'tun	4.5m N Truro off A30	House on grassland.

Detail: Georgian house. Gardens (open on application)

Chiverton Cross	CHIV'r'tun Cross	5m NW Truro on A390	Named after house on grassland

Detail: Major roundabout also known as Three Burrows.

Chy Vogue	Shy VO'g	5m SW Truro off A39	Furnace house
Clodgy	CLOD'gi	in E Helston	Leper house/hospital
Clowance	CLOW'ans (as in 'now')	3.5m SW Camborne off B3303	Meadow

Details: Holiday complex. House originally owned by St. Aubyn family. Three Cornish crosses in grounds.

Coads Green dating	CODES Green	5m SW Launceston on B3257	Code is a local name from 17C/18C

Detail: Holy well of All Hallows at Higher Trefrize 1.5m E near site of chapel.

Cober River	CO'ber River	Rises near Carthew, goes through Helston to Loe Pool	Brook (from Gover)
Cockwells	Cockwells	4m NE Penzance on A30	From person called Cockwel, 1755
Colan	KO'len	3m E Newquay off A392	From patron saint St. Colan

Details: Saint has links with Wales and Brittany.Church, 13C 15C, restored 1879, 1884, was given to Glasney College in 1276, has 14C S doorway,rood screen base, brasses of 1572, 1575. Cornish Cross. Holy well of our Lady of Nance .5m S of church, famous for curing sore eyes and foretelling the future.

Coldrenick	Cul'DREN'ick	3.5m SE Liskeard off A38	Thorny place
Colliford Lake	KOLLY'fud Lake	9m NE Bodmin off A30	Cool ford, from nearby farms of Colliford.

Details: 900 acre reservoir provides fishing,walking, birdwatching. Loveny nature reserve.

Colquite	Kol'QUITE	3m NW Bodmin off B3266	Ridged back wood

Details: 15C ruin below manor house. Cornish Cross in garden.

Come-To-Good	Cum-to-good	3.5m S Truro off B3289	Valley of house in wood.

Details: Quaker Friends Meeting House, built 1710, has thatched roof and covered stables.

Comford	KUM'fut	2.5m SE Redruth on A393	Crooked way in valley
Common Moor	Common Moor	3.5m N Liskeard off B3254	Moor at end of Siblyback Lake

Detail: Village founded 1867

Quaker Meeting House at Come-to-Good

Comprigney	**Cum'PRIG'ni**	NW fringe of Truro on B3284	Bell beams or Gallowtrees field
Condurrow	**Kn'DER'a**	1m S Camborne off A3047	Waters meet
Congdon's Shop	**CONG'dns Shop**	5m SW Launceston on B3254	Congdon's workshop
Connor Downs	**KONNA Downs**	2.5m E Hayle off A30	19C village on former downland, named after former manor of Connerton.
Constantine	**CONS'tan'tine or Cos'TEN'ten (archaic)**	5m SW Falmouth, S of A394	After St. Constantine

Details: He was said to be a 6C king and martyr. Tall impressive church, 15C 16C, restored 1862 & later, has rood screen, carved panels 1520, sedilia,stoup, 200 kneelers, 1574 brass is palimpsest with 14C Flemish knight on reverse, brass 1616. Cornish cross, and another 1.75m NNW at Trevease Farm. Polwheveral Bridge 1572.

Constantine Bay	**Con'stan'tine Bay**	3.5m W Padstow off B3276	From nearby 14C St. Constantine's Chapel dedicated to saintly King of Cornwall.

Details: Holy well of St. Constantine .5m N, once ringed by seats where pilgrims prayed to bring on rain after drought

Coombe	**Coom**	4m N Bude off A39	Valley
Combe	**Coom**	.75m SW Callington off A390	Valley
Coombe	**Coom**	5m W St. Austell off A390	Valley
Coombe Kea	**Coom Key**	2.5m SE Truro off A39	Valley of Kea

Coosebean	COOZ'been	NW fringe of Truro off A39	Little wood
Coppathorne	COP'a'thorn	3.5m S Bude on A39	Pollarded (copped) thorn trees
Copperhouse	COPPER'house	adjoining Hayle off A30	Copper smelting works

Detail: Engine house of first steam railway in Cornwall built 1834

Cornelly	Corn'ELLY	7.5m E Truro off A3078	After St. Cornelius, Pope and Bishop of Rome. AD 253.

Details: Saint venerated as a martyr and patron of horned beasts. Isolated church, 13C, restored 1886 & 1900, wagon roof in porch, pulpit 17C, monuments to Gregor family of Trewarthenick, including William, d 1817, who discovered the mineral manaccanite, later called titanium. (See entry under Manaccan).

Cornwall Coast Path Corn'wull (not CornWALL) Nearly 300 miles from Marsland Mouth on North coast to Cremyll on South coast
Details: From Kernow "The Horn people" from position as peninsular.

Cosawes	K'SAWZ	2.5m NW Penryn off A393	Englishmen's wood

Details: A chapel to St. Mary Magdalene, which was a shrine and pilgrimage place in Middle Ages, once stood in Chapel Close. Workings of 17C & 18C Magdalen Bal nearby.

Costislost	Cost'i'lost	2.5m SE Wadebridge off A389	Farm which did not make good, or English nickname for a poor field
Coswarth	Cos'WARTH	3.5m SE Newquay off A392	Upper wood
Cot Valley	Cot Valley	.5m SW St.Just off A3071	Short valley (was Porth Nanven - bay valley).
Cotehele	Co'TEEL	6m N Saltash off A390	Wood on an estuary.

Details: Exceptional medieval house, garden, mill, chapel on cliff and quay. National Trust. National Maritime Museum Outstation.

Couch's Mill	Cooch's Mill	2.5m E Lostwithiel off A390	After local family?
Coverack	CUV'rak	2m SW St.Keverne on B3294	Cove at streams place
Coverack Bridges	CUV'rak Bridges	2m NE Helston off B3297	Streams place
Cow and Calf Rocks	Cow and Calf Rocks	off Port Quinn 5.5m NW Wadebridge	Probably from shape of rocks
Cowlands	COW'lunds	2.5m S Truro off B3289	Steep-sided valley
Crackington Haven	Crackington Hayven (locally Cracken Awn)	8m SW Bude off A39	Harbour at Crack, from Manor of Crackington.
Crafthole	CRAFT'ole	5m W Torpoint off A374	Croft hill with enclosed arable land.

Detail: Local saying in Crafthole "twelve houses and thirteen cuckolds".

Crane Islands	Crane Islands	3.m NW Camborne, W of Portreath	Hill fort
Crankan	Cran'ken	3m N Penzance off B3311	Fort of grief. Courtyard houses nr Chysauster
Crantock	CRAN'tock	1.5m SW Newquay off A3075	From St. Carantoc

Details: The saint,of Welsh royal birth, tamed a dragon on his way to Cornwall. Church,Norman & later (collegiate in 13C with dean and 10 prebendaries), central tower collapsed 1412, another built at west end, restoration 1899 by Sedding, has rood screen mostly modern, 18C communion rails, 15C sculpture inside tower, stocks. Holy well of St. Crantock in village centre. Holy Well of St. Ambrusca NW of church. Port in 13C.

Creed	Kreed	7m SW St. Austell off A390	From female St. Crida

Details: The saint is said to be either the daughter of tribal chief Mark, or of Irish King Leinster. Church dedicated to St. Andrew, 13C, 15C, restored 1904, has Norman pillar piscina with 13C niche, font 13C, chancel piscina 14C, wagon roof, rood screen, slate memorials, 1570, 1602, commandment boards, photo of Titanium Bowl and record of William Gregor's disovery of titanium(Gregor was a former rector).

Creegbrawse	Creeg'brawse	4m E Redruth off A390	Great barrow
Crellow	CRELL'o	4m NW Penryn, near Stithians, off A393	Ancient round
Cremyll	CREM'ill	1.5m SE Torpoint on B3247	The hill
Cribba Head	CREE'ba Head	2m SW St. Buryan off B3315	Crests or reefs
Criggan	CRIG'un	5m N St.Austell off A391	Small mound or barrow
Crinnis	CRIN'is	1.5m SE St. Austell off A390	Camp settlement on the island, or Lambs' fort
Cripples' Ease	Cripples' Ease	2.5m SW St. Ives on B3311	19C hamlet at top of a long hill
Crockett	Crock'it	2m N Callington off B3257	Hazel tree wood
Crofthandy	Croft'ANDY	2.5m E Redruth off B3298	Rough pasture with ruins of old house
Crowan	CROW'un (as in now)	4.5m NW Helston off B3303	from St. Crewenna

Details: The saint is thought to have come from Ireland with St.Breage,landing at Hayle. Church, 15C, 16C, restored 1870, has N. aisle with angels bearing shields, brasses to St. Aubyn family 1400-1599 & Adam tablet.

Crowdy Reservoir	CROW'dy Reservoir	2m E Camelford off A39	On site of Crowdy Marsh (hovels on the marsh).
Crowlas	CROW'luss (as in now)	3m NE Penzance on A30	Hovel by a ford
Crowntown	Crowntown	2.5m NW Helston on B3303	Hill town?
Crows An Wra	Crowse (as in now) an RAY	1.5m NW St. Buryan on A30	Hags or witch's cross
Crow's Nest	Crow's Nest	3.5m NE Liskeard off B3254	High fort
Crow Sound	Crow Sound	NE of St. Mary's, Isles of Scilly	Sailable channel, from Crow Rock
Crugmeer	Crug'MEAR	1.5m NW Padstow off B3276	Great barrow
Crumplehorn	Crump'l'horn	.5m N Polperro on A387	Maelhoern's farm
Cubert	Kew'bert	3m SW Newquay off A3075	From St. Cubertus

Details: The Welsh saint is sometimes confused with St. Cuthbert of Lindisfarne. Church, 14C, 15C, has broach spire rebuilt 1852 by Street after lightning damage, wagon roofs, unusual Norman font, pulpit made from bench ends, early inscribed stone in tower wall, slate memorials 1669, 1699. Cornish Cross.Holy Well of St.Cubert 1m NW, another in cave at Holy Well Bay

Cuby	Kew'bee	6m E Truro off A3078	After St. Cuby.

Details: Revered Cornish born saint, fathered by St. Levan. His missionary work took him to Wales where he founded a monastery at Holyhead.Church, now parish church of Tregony, has 14C tower, 16C porch, rebuilt 1828, restored 1899, S.porch has king heads as bosses and label stops, early inscribed stone in S. aisle. Holy Well of St. Cuby S of church.

Cuddra	CUD'ra	1.5m E St. Austell off A390	Wooded estate

Culdrose	Culd'ROSE	1.5m S Helston off A3083	Moor or high land nook

Details: Western Europe's largest helicopter station. Flambards village.

Cury	CURE'i	4m SE Helston off A3083	After St. Corentius, a Breton, first Bishop of Cornouaille.

Details: Church, Norman,14C 15C,restored 1873, has Norman S door, squint.Tall wheel Cornish cross in churchyard.The Rev. Sandys Wason,1905-19,was deprived of the living for his extreme Catholic practices.

Cury Cross Lanes	KURE'ee Cross Lanes	4.5m SE Helston on A3083	Cross roads (see previous entry) lying between Bochym and Bonython Manors
Cusgarne	Cuss'GARN	5m SW Truro off A393	Crane's wood
Cutmere	CUT'mear	6m SE Liskeard off A38	Great wood

D

Darite	D'right	3m N Liskeard off B3254	From family of Daryth?

Detail: In 1900 called Railway Terrace.

Davidstow	DAVID'stoe or Dewstow	3.5m NE Camelford on A395	Holy place of St. David, patron saint of Wales.

Details: The church at nearby Altarnun is dedicated to his mother, St. Nonn. Church, 15C, rebuilt & drastically restored 1875, has carved bench ends, including bagpiper, and slate monuments. Charlotte Dymond, murdered in 1844, buried in churchyard. Davidstowe Holy well NE of church. Airfield in World War 2, then used as race circuit where Lotus had first F1 victory. Prize-winning cheddar cheese made at local creamery.

Daw's House	Door's House	1.5m SW Launceston on B3254	After Daw family?
Degibna	D'GIB'na	2m S Helston off A3083 near Loe Pool	From St. Degiman, whose chapel was nearby
Delabole	Del'a'BOWL	2m W Camelford on B3314	Pit at Delyou

Details: Famous slate quarry with viewing platform and display room. St. John's Church 1880 and Methodist Chapel 1863.

De Lank River	De LANK River	Bodmin Moor off A30	From Dymlanke a holding of land. Possibly ravine fort.

Details: De Lank quarry, .75m S of St. Breward, supplied granite for new London Bridge

Demelza	D'MEL'za	6m SW Bodmin off A30	Maeldaf's fort.

Detail: Winston Graham named one of the main characters in his "Poldark" series after this place.

Dennis Head	Dennis Head	3m N St. Keverne off B3293	Hill fort

Details: Camp fortresses here since Iron Age. In mid-17C, 100 men stationed in castle, of which only banks & earthworks remain.

Devichoys	DEV'e'choice	2m W Penryn on A39	Sheep wood or Burnt wood.
Deviock	Dev'ee'ock	4m E Looe off A387	Not known

Detail: Holy well of Tregonnick .5m NE of village

Devoran	DEV'ran	4m SW Truro off A39	Waters where three streams merge into creek.

Details: St. John's church 1856 by J.L. Pearson, Truro Cathedral architect, has memorial to Lobb brothers, famous plant collectors, who lived in area

Dinhams Bridge	DIN'hams Bridge	2.5m NE Wadebridge off A39	Small fort
Dizzard	DIZ'ud	5m SW Bude off A39	Very steep place
Dobwalls	DOB'walls	2.5m W Liskeard on A38	Dobb's walls, after local family named Dobbe. Alternatively Hogswall (pig's wall)

Detail: Family Adventure Park.

Doddycross	Doddy'CROSS	3.5m SE Liskeard off A38	Personal name?
Dodman Point	DUD'man Point	4m S Mevagissey	From local family of Dudman/ Dudemann?

Details: Headland 373ft high, with granite cross. Iron Age cliff castle.

Dolcoath	DOLL'coath (to rhyme with 'both')	at Pool near Camborne	Old ground or hole.
Doniert Stone	DON'yert Stone	3m NW Liskeard N of St. Cleer	Personal name

Detail: By road, cross base with inscription meaning 'Doniert ordered this cross for the good of his soul'.

Dorminack	Door'MINE'uk	2.5m SE St. Buryan, near Lamorna Cove, off B3315	Stony ground.

Detail: House where authors Derek and Jeannie Tangye lived.

Doublebois	DOUBLE'boys	4m W Liskeard off A38	From Fr. double wood or two woods
Downderry	Down'DERRI	4m E Looe on B3247	Obscure.

Detail: Could be from English dun (hill) or Irish dun (fort)

Downgate	Down'GATE	2m N Callington off B3257	Gate leading onto downs
Downgate	Down'GATE	4.5m NE Liskeard on B3254	Gate leading onto downs
Dozmary Pool	DOZ'm'ree	9m NE Bodmin off A30	In 1300 'a lake at the top of Tosmeri hill'.

Details: The water is said to rise and fall like the tides. As a punishment John Tregeagle had to drain it with a limpet shell. Great revel there in 1773.

Drakewalls	DRAKE'walls	4m SW Tavistock on A390	Link with Drake family?
Draynes Bridge	Drains Bridge	3.5m NW Liskeard off A38 on River Fowey	Thorny place
Drift Reservoir	Drift Reservoir	2.5m W Penzance off A30	The village or settlement (in 1262 Little Drift).

Detail: Reservoir constructed 1961.

Drinnick	DRIN'ick	5m NW St. Austell nr Nanpean off B3279	Thorny place
Drym	Drim	4.5m NW Helston off B3302	Ridge
Duloe	Dew'LOW	3m NW Looe on B3254 off A38	Between the two Rivers Looe

Details: Church, dedicated to St. Cuby (see entry under "Cuby")and St. Leonard, 13C, 15C, restored 1861-3, has piers with good carved capitals, parclose screen, stoup, effigy of Sir John Colshull 1483 in chapel and other interesting slate monuments. Holy well of St. Cuby in granite building .5m E, and stone circle of eight stones nearby.

Dunheved	Dun'HEV'ed	in S Launceston off A30	Chief hill

Detail: Old name for Launceston

Dunmere	DUN'mear	2m NW Bodmin on A389, near River Camel	Great fort
Dupath	Doo'puth	.75m SE Callington off A388	Thieves path

Detail: Holy well in 16C building. Cornwall Heritage Trust.

Duporth	Doo'PORTH	1m SE St. Austell off A390	Two coves
Durfold	DER'fold Locally Durl	5.5m NE Bodmin off A30 E of Blisland	Sheep enclosure near water
Durgan	DUR'gun	4m SW Falmouth near River Helford	Water by downs
Dutson	DUTS'un	1m NE Launceston on A388	Not known

E

Eastcott	Est'cut	7.5m NE Bude off A39	East cottage
East Looe	East Loo	opposite West Looe off A387	Pool or inlet.

Details: Church of St. Mary rebuilt by Street 1851. Chapel of St. Anne, rebuilt 1805 and 1882. Old Guildhall and 17C houses, Museum. Shark museum. Holy well of St. Mary. Bridge of 13 arches built early 15C connected two Looes.

East Taphouse	East TAP'house	4.5m W Liskeard on A390	Ale house
Eathorne	EE'thorn	4m SW Falmouth off A39	Furze
Eddystone Rocks	EDDY'stun Rocks	5m S Torpoint off B3247	Eddy stone or sea currents around rocks
Eden Project	Eden Project	at Bodelva 1m W St. Blazey off A390	A garden of Eden

Details: Global garden project in giant geodesic structures in old china clay pit, founded by Tim Smit and Cornish architect Jonathon Ball, former Vice President of the RIBA, in 1994.

Edgcumbe	EDGE'cum	5m W Falmouth on A394	After Edgcumbe family
Edmonton	Ed'mun'tun	1.5m NW Wadebridge off A39	Eadhelm's estate ?
Egloshayle	Egloss-HAYLE	.5m E Wadebridge off A389	Church on estuary (Cornish for estuary is 'hayl')

Details: Thought to be dedicated to St. Conan, who was either an associate of St. Petroc or the first bishop of Athelstan's foundation at St. Germans. Church, 13C 15C, restored 1867, has wagon roof,15C stone pulpit, slate memorial 1581,marble bust to Dame Barbara Molesworth 1735. Holy well of St. Wenna at Trenance Mill. Two Cornish crosses in churchyard.

Egloskerry	Eglo'SKERRY	3.5m NW Launceston off B3254	Church (eglos) of Keri.

Details: The female saint St. Keri was one of the 24 children of Broccan. Church, Norman, 15C, restored 1887, has Norman N wall & transept, rare piscina, 14C effigy, slate memorials 1624,1742. Holy well S of ch.

Egypt	Egypt	3m NW Callington off A388 W of Golberdon	Named after visit to that country?
Ellenglaze	Ell'in'GLASE	3.5m SW Newquay off A3075 nr Penhale Sands	Green corner
Engollen	N'GOLL'n	4.5m SW Padstow off B3276	Old hazel trees
Enniscaven	Ennis'CAV'n or Ennis'scawn?	5.5m NW St. Austell off A30 (edge of Goss Moor)	Remote place with elder tree
Enys	EN'iss	1.5m NE Penryn of A39	Land insulated by streams or roads.

Details: House 1833 by Henry Harrison. Bluebell garden, ponds, waterwheel

Erisey	Rizzy or Er'IS'ee?	4m NE Lizard off A3083	Acre

F

River Fal	River Fal	enters Carrick Roads near Feock and winds NE	

through Tregony to Grampound and beyond. Name is obscure, may be pre-Celtic - 'sun or river god'

Falmouth	FAL'muth	at end of A39	Mouth of the Fal

Details: Previously known as Smitheck ('smiths' village) & Penny-come-quick. Pendennis Castle built by Henry VIII. Packet ships in 17C, 18C & early 19C. Town docks from 1860. Kenneth Grahame wrote much of "Wind In The Willows" at Greenbank Hotel. Arwennack House 16C, parish church 1664 with later additions, St. Michael's Church, Penwerris, 1827. Custom House and Polytechnic 1833. Art gallery, Art Centre, National Maritime Museum. Home to Tall Ships Festival. Annual Falmouth Week (yacht racing) and Oyster Festival. Leisure Centre. Three main beaches. Deep anchorage. Tourist Office: 28 Killigrew St. 01326-312300

Farms Common	Farms Common	4m N Helston on B3297	Common surrounded by farms
Faugan	FORE'gn	SW fringe of Newlyn off A30	Cave
Fentonwanson	Fen'tun'ONE'sn	near St. Teath 3m SW Camelford off A39	Spring
Fentonadle	Fentun'AD'le	1m NW St. Breward off B3266	Spring - St. Adwena's well

Details: The saint was one of the daughters of King Broccan, sometimes called St. Anne or St. Tane. Holy well .25m S

Fentongollan	Fentun'GOLL'n	2.5m SE Truro off A3078	Spring by hazel tree

Details: Holy well of Fentongollan .75m SW (ancient manor of Fentongollan rebuilt at Tregothnan)

Fentongoose	Fen'tun'GOOS	3m SW Truro off A390	Spring of the wood
Fentonladock	Fen'tun'LAD'uck	6m NE Truro off B3275	Spring

Detail: Well is .5m NE of Ladock

Fentonluna	Fen'tun'LOON'a	in N Padstow	Spring by pools

Detail: Holy well of Fenton Luna SE of Prideaux Place.

Feock	FEE'ock	4m S Truro off A39	From St. Feoca or perhaps St. Fiacre (Irish hermit).

Details: The saint founded churches in Brittany. Church, 15C, enlarged 1846, rebuilt 1874, has unusual Norman font, pulpit with 16C Flemish panels,stocks, 13C separate tower, lych gate and Cornish Cross. Last service in Cornish language said to have been held here. Holy well in Halvarras Road built over.

Fiddlers Green	Fiddlers Green	4m S Newquay off A30	Not known
Fire Beacon Point	Fire Beacon Point	4.5m NW Camelford off B3263	Location of fire beacon
Fistral	FIST'rul	1m W Newquay off A392	Obscure
Fivelanes	Five Lanes	8m SW Launceston off A30	Meeting of five turnings
Fletchers Bridge	Fletchers Bridge	2.5m E Bodmin off A38	Named after Fletcher family?

Detail: Bodmin Farm Park.

Flexbury	Flex'bry	1m N Bude off A39	Hill where flax grows
Flushing	Flushing	.5m N Falmouth (by ferry) off A39	After Vlissingen in Holland

Details: Previously known as Nankersey (nans kersey, reed bed valley). 18C houses, fashionable for Packet service captains. Church of St. Peter 1842 has organ from Exeter Hall, London, fragment of ancient sculpture and Burne-Jones/Morris window. Cornish cross in churchyard found by the Rev. Forbes Savage in 1891 in a pigstye, having formerly been used as the base of a threshing machine.

Forder	Forder	SW fringe of Saltash off A38	Paths
Forrabury	For'a'bry	S edge of Boscastle off B3263	Paths by a fortified place

Details: Church, dedicated to St. Symphorian (see entry under Veryan), Norman, 15C, 1760 tower, restored 1868, has Norman S wall & transept, bench ends in pulpit & altar. Cornish cross S of churchyard.

Four Lanes	FOUR Lanes	2.5m SW Redruth on B3297	Cross road of four turnings in 19C mining village

Parish church at Fowey
overlooking the river

Fowey	FOY	6m E St. Austell on A3082	Beech trees river (town named after river).

Details: Said to be dedicated to Irish abbot-bishop, St. Finbarr (also known as Barry), or St. Barry, one of the 24 children of King Broccan. Later re-dedicated to St. Nicholas. Church 14C, 15C, restored 1876, has richly decorated 4-storey tower, carved wagon roof, clerestory pulpit 1601(said to come from cabin of Spanish galleon), porch with groined ceiling, brasses 1450,1582,1601,other Rashleigh monuments of 1610 & 1683.Place House has Porphyry Hall Medieval houses and inns, almshouses 17C,Town Hall 1792.Du Maurier Literary Centre, Town Museum, Noah's Ark Museum, St. Catherines' Castle. "Q" Memorial. Tourist Office: 4 Custom House Hill. 01726-833616

Foxhole	FOX'ole	4m NW St. Austell on B3279	Name of an old tin works 'fox's hole', transferred to village in 1748.

Detail: Watch Hill nearby has five tumuli

Fraddam	FRAD'un	2.5m SE Hayle off B3302	Small stream?
Fraddon	FROD'an	7m SE Newquay off A30	Place of streams
Fradgan	FRAD'jan	in Newlyn off A30	Ox road? Also Street-an-Nowan in Newlyn (ox street)
Freathy	FREETH'y	3m SW Torpoint off B3247	After Fredea or Fridia family in area 14C & earlier?
Frogpool	FROG'pool	5m SW Truro off A393	Frog pools

36

G

Garras	**GA'rus** (hard 'g', short 'a')	3.5m SE Helston off B3293	Rough moorland

<u>Detail:</u> 18C village built on common grazing land, originally rough moorland

Garrow Tor	**Garro TAW**	4m SE Camelford off A30	Rough moorland, or possibly after Garra family.
Gear	**Gear**	1.5m N Penzance off B3311	A fort or round (other spellings elsewhere are Geer and Geor).
Geevor Mine	**GEE'ver** (hard 'g' as in got)	.75m W Pendeen off B3306	From early tin work called the goat's tinstream.

<u>Details:</u> Tin mining museum. Levant Beam Engine.

Georgia	**Jorja**	3m SW St. Ives off B3311	Low or broken down hedge
Germoe	**GER'mo** (G as in got)	5.5m W Helston on A394	Dedicated to St. Germoch

<u>Details:</u> He was an Irish king, who came with St. Breaca, landing at Hayle. Church, Norman, 14C 15C, restored 1860, 1891, has Norman W window, chancel & S transept walls; 14C S windows & N aisle; 15C S porch with crucifix, stoup. King Germoe's Chair, 15C in churchyard has three seats. Holy well of St. Germoe SW of church.

Gernick	**GERN'ick** (hard 'g')	2.5m S Camborne off B3303	Stony place
Gerrans	**GE'runs** (hard G)	7m SE Truro off A3078	Believed named from St. Gerent

<u>Details:</u> He was a king and member of important Cornish family tracing from Lud, St. Gerrent, St. Erbyn, St. Just, St. Selevan to St. Cuby. Church, 14C 15C, rebuilt 1849 by William White, has rare octagonal spire, piscina, bench ends, stoup. Fine Cornish Cross.

Gilbert's Coombe	**Gilbert's Coom**	1m N Redruth on B3300	After Gilbert family?
Gillan	**GILL'in**	2.5m N St. Keverne off B3293	Creek
Glasney	**GLAZ'nee**	in Penryn off A39	Green place
Glendurgan	**Glen'DER'gn**	.5m SW Mawnan Smith off A39	Deep valley by river

<u>Details:</u> Gardens, maze and Giant's Stride. Fox family/National Trust.

Gloweth	**GLOW'eth** (to rhyme with HOW)	2m W Truro off A390	Clear stream or charcoal wood
Glynn	**Glin**	3m SE Bodmin off A38 on River Fowey	Deep valley

<u>Details:</u> Glynn House built 1805. Cornish crosses in grounds.

Godolphin	**G'DOLL'fin**	4.5m NW Helston off B3280	Obscure - little hillock suggested

<u>Details:</u> 15C, 16C, 17C house & garden, Schofield family/Nat.Trust.

Godolphin Cross	**G'DOLL'fin cross**	4m NW Helston off B3280	19C village at cross roads
Godrevy	**Gud'REEV'i**	4m NE Hayle off B3301 on Godrevy Point	Smallholdings

<u>Details:</u> Godrevy Island Lighthouse 1859 off Godrevy Point on which Virginia Woolf based her novel "To The Lighthouse"

Golant	**G'LANT**	7m E St. Austell off B3269 on River Fowey	Feast or field of the valley

Details: Church dedicated to St. Samson, a Welsh noble abbot-bishop who founded monasteries in Cornwall, Ireland & Brittany & was the leading churchman in the evangilisation of Cornwall and the Channel Islands. On his way to the continent he converted a group paying honour to an idol with a play, music and dancing. Church, 16C, restored 1842, has carved & inscribed wagon and cradle roofs, 18C box pews, pulpit & stalls of interesting bench ends, 15C stained glass. Holy well of St. Sampson near S. porch. (See also South Hill).

Golberdon	**GOLL'ber'dun**	2.5m NW Callington off A388	Hill, downland. Golber's farm.

Detail: 18C village built on rough grazing land.

Golden	**Golden**	5.5m NE Truro off A3078	Fair, festival or field?

Details: Manor has traces of hall house and barn with original cruck roof timbers. Cuthbert Mayne, was discovered at Golden and hung, drawn and quartered as a Roman Catholic martyr. Holy well to E.

Goldsithney	**Gol'SITH'nee**	4.5m E Penzance on B3280 near Helston.	Fair (goel) of St. Sithney,
Golitha Falls	**G'LEETH'a Falls**	3.5m NW Liskeard off A38	Overflowing

Details: Two 19C wheelpits from Wheal Victoria survive. Nature reserve.

Gonvena	**Gon'VEEN'a**	Northern fringe of Wadebridge off A39	White hill
Goodagrane	**GOODY'grain**	2.5m SW Penryn off A394	Crane's lair or watercourse
Goonabarn	**Goon'a'BARN**	4m NW St. Austell off B3279	Top of the downs
Goonamarris	**Goon'a'MARRIS** (short 'a')	4.5m NW St. Austell off B3279	The horse downs
Goonbell	**Goon'BELL**	.5m SE St. Agnes off B3277	Far downs

Detail: Village founded 1813

Goon Gumpus	**Goon GUMP'us**	3m E Redruth off B3298	Level downs
Goonhavern	**Gun'HAV'ern**	5m SW Newquay off A3075	Downs of summer fallow land
Goonhilly Downs	**Gun'ILL'ee Downs**	6m SE Helston on B3293	Hunting downs.

Detail: Post Ofice Earth station & visitor centre

Goonlaze	**Goon'LAYZE**	3.5m SE Redruth off B3297 near Stithians Lake	Green downs
Goonlaze	**Goon'LAYZE**	E fringe of St. Agnes on B3285	Green downs
Goonamarth	**Goon'a'MARTH**	2.5m NW St. Austell off A3058	Horse downs
Goonown	**Goon'OWN** (as in clown)	1m SE St. Agnes off B3277	Downs
Goon Piper	**Goon PIPER**	3m S Truro off B3289	Piper's downs
Goonreeve	**Goon'REEV**	3m NW Penryn off A393	Red downs
Goonvrea	**Goon'VRAY**	1m SW St. Agnes off B3277	Hill downs
Gooseham	**GOOS'um**	7m NW Bude off A39	Goose meadow
Gorran	**GORR'n** (Gurran in 1699)	6.5m SW St. Austell off B3273	After St. Guron

Details: The saint was originally at Bodmin (holy well named after him). Church, 13C,15c, restored 1874, has 90ft tower, wagon roof,piscina,53 bench ends, coffin slab, brass 1510.

Gorran Haven	**GORR'n Haven**	7m S St. Austell B3273	Harbour of St. Gorran

Details: Formerly Porthjust, then Portheast (East is another pronunciation of Just, to whom the chapel is dedicated). Chapel 15C, restored 1885,has five-sided tower.

Goscott	Gos'cut	1m SW Week St. Mary	Short wood?
Goss Moor	GOSS Moor	6m nw St. Austell off A30	Moor with wood
Gover Valley	GO'ver Valley	1.5m NW St. Austell off A3058	Brook valley
Goverrow	G'VEH'ra	3m SE Redruth off A393	Streams
Grade	Grade	.5m W Cadgwith off A3083	From St. Grada, possibly same as St. Crida of Creed.

Details: Church in isolated position, mainly Norman, rebuilt 1862, has brass to James Erisey & family 1522. Holy well of serpentine .5m NE dedicated to St. Ruan, whose remains were in a shrine at Tavistock Abbey until Reformation.

Grambler	GRAM'bler	.5m E Redruth off A393	Dolmen, quoit

Detail: Wheal Grambler mine, now a farm

Grampound	GRAM'pound	7m SW St. Austell off A390	Great bridge (from Fr. grand pont) crossing River Fal.

Details: In 13C called Ponsmur. Chapel of St. Nunn rebuilt 1869 on 14C site of chapel of St. Mary. Medieval cross 12ft. Holy well of St. Naunter .5m n at Trevillick. Garden at The Hollies.

Grampound Rd	GRAM'pound Rd	8m SW St. Austell off A390	(See previous entry).

Detail: 19C village which grew up round railway station

Great Arthur	Great Arthur	Isles of Scilly 2m NE St. Mary's	From personal name

Details: On highest point of Great Arthur is a round barrow; on Middle Arthur are two entrance graves and on Little Arthur five entrance graves.

Greeb Point	Greeb Point	2m E St. Mawes off A3078	Crest or ridge
Green Bottom	Green Bott'um	4m W Truro off A390	Low ground (English)
Greensplatt	Green'splatt	4m SW Truro off A39	Plot of land (splat)
Greenwith Common	Green'with (to rhyme with kith) Common	4m SW Truro off A39	Dry trees (from 'gwyth')
Gregwartha	Greg'WA'tha	2.5m S Redruth off B3297	Higher barrow or hill
Greystone Bridge	Gray'stun Bridge	3.5m SE Launceston on B3362	Bridge of grey stones

Detail: Has five arches, built 1439.

Gribbin Head	Grib'n Head	5.5m SE St. Austell off A3082	Little ridge, or possibly named after a local family
Grimscott	Grims'cut	3m E Bude on B3254	Grim's cottage
Grogoth Wollas	GRO'gath Wallus	6m E Truro off A3078	Lower place
Grumbla	GRUM'bla	4m W Penzance off A30	Dolmen

Detail: Megalithic remains nearby

Gugh	G'YOO island	2m SW St. Mary's, Isles of Scilly	Hedge banks

Details: On N end of island on Kittern Hill are ten round barrows, with two other tombs on the S hill of the island.

Gulland Rock	GULL'und Rock	3.5m NW Padstow near Padstow Bay	Gull rock
Gulval	GUL'vl	1m NE Penzance off B3311	After obscure female saint Wolvela (Cornish form probably Gwelvel)

Details: Also suggested St. Gudwal, a monk well known in Brittany, but born on the British coast. Church, built 1440, restored 1892,has 13C font, piscina & credence, 14C cherub's head, sundial on porch. The Rev. William Wingfield was vicar for nearly 74 years (1839-1913). Inscribed stones S. of churchyard and at Barlowena Bottom. Cornish cross shaft mistakenly mounted upside down. Holy well nearby has interesting history and legends. Iron Age hut circles and courtyard houses in area.

Gummows Shop   **Gummowes Shop** 4m SE Newquay   Small or tributary valley
off A3058

Gunnislake   **GUNNIS'lake**   5m NE Callington on   Gunna's stream, or
A390 by River Tamar   worked out place in
mine by a stream.

Details: 19C village grew up round mines. Church 1881.The New Bridge, built 1520, seven arches, best of all Cornish granite bridges (Pevsner) .Tamar Valley railway line terminus. Tamar Valley Donkey Park. Morwellham Quay to S.

Gunver Head   **GUN'va Head**   2m NW Padstow   Obscure possibly
downs on headland,
with dramatic chasm at
cliff's foot

Gunwalloe   **Gn'WAL'o**   3m S Helston off A3083   After St. Winwaloe

Details: Patron saint, born in Brittany. His mother is said to have grown another breast after having triplets. As a child he restored his sister's eye after it was swallowed by a goose. Church, rebuilt 14C-15C, restored 1869, has wagon roofs, rood screen painted panels of apostles, stoup, tower of earlier church, built into rock, stands on own. Cornish Cross. Holy well used to be near detached tower.

Gurnard's Head   **Gernards Head** 5.5m W St. Ives off B3306 Shaped like head of a
gurnard fish.

Details: Cliff castle. Also known as The Isnarl or desolate place. Remains of Chapel Jane nearby.

Gwarnick Mill   **GWOR'nick Mill** 2.5m N Truro off B3284 Alder grove or marsh

Gwealavellan   **GWEEL'a'vell'un** 3m NE Hayle off B3301   Mill in open field

Gweek   **Gweek**   3m SE Helston off A394, Village in a forest
top of River Helford

Detail: Seal Sanctuary

Gwennap   **GWEN'up**   3m SE Redruth off A393 From St. Wenappa.

Detail: She may be St. Wynup in list of 24 sons and daughters of King Broccan of Breconshire. Church, 15C, rebuilt 1862-1891, has detached tower with pyramidal roof, piscina, tablet by Neville Northey Burnard. Cornish cross in Vicarage garden and shaft of cross buried in vestry foundations or building. Holy well 600 yds E of church.

Gwennap Pit   **GWEN'up Pit** 1m SE Redruth off A393 From St. Wenappa.

Details: Stepped grass amphitheatre where Wesley preached from 1743 to 1762. Annual open air services held. Museum of Cornish Methodism at Carharrack.

Gwenter   **GWIN'ta**   4m SW St. Keverne   Windy or white land or
off B3293   fair water

Gwinear   **GWIN'ear**   2m E Hayle off A30   From St. Fingar or
St. Gwinear

Details: The saint is said to be son of an Irish king, martyred in Cornwall with 777 companions by Cornish pagan King Theodoric. After being beheaded Gwinear is said to have picked up his head and walked away with it. Church, 13C, 14C restored 1881,has early Decorated chancel window, piscina, pulpit, lectern & kneeling desk of bench ends including merman, rood screen. Two Cornish crosses. NE is Holy well of Gwinear Roseworthy.

Gwithian   **GWITH'ee'un** 2.5m NE Hayle on B3301 From little known
St. Gothian

Details: The oratory to him is buried in the sands. Also known as church of Connartona from lost manor of Connerton. Church, 15C, rebuilt 1866 by Sedding, retaining tower. Cornish cross in churchyard. Bronze Age farm excavated at Gwithian Towans .5m N, but not now visible. 1m N at Crane Godrevy ruins of small manor of 11-17C. 1m NE near Sand Cot Holy well of St. Gwithian.

Gyllyngdune   **Gilling'DUNE** in S Falmouth   Deep inlet

Gyllyngvase   **Gilling'VAZE** in S Falmouth   Shallow inlet

Bob Fitzsimmons's cottage in Helston.

Born in Helston, the son of a policeman, Bob Fitzsimmons became the world boxing champion at Heavy-Weight, Middle-Weight and Light-Heavyweight. In 1891 he beat Jack Dempsey by a knock-out in the 14th round to become world middleweight champion. In 1896 he knocked out Peter Maher in America in 95 seconds for the world heavyweight title. The former heavyweight champion Gentleman Jim Corbett, came out of retirement and met Fitzsimmons in 1897. The Fighting Blacksmith as he was known, landed his famous solar plexus knockout punch in the 14th round. In 1903 he was challenged by 26 year old George Gardiner in the light heavyweight division. After a long and gruelling fight he won on points in the 20th round.

H

Halabezack	Hal'a'BEZ'eck	4.5m S Redruth off B3297	Midge infested marsh
Halgabron	Hal'GAB'run	1m E Tintagel off B3263	Gabran's marsh
Halgavor	Hal'GAY'ver	2m S Bodmin off B3268	Goat's marsh
Halliggye	Hall'IG'ee	4m SE Helston off B3293	Willow groves

Detail: Fogou near Iron Age round

| Hallworthy | HALL'worth'i | 6m ne Camelford on A395 | Gorgi's marsh, formerly Halldrunkard, not because near an inn, but Haldronket "marsh by a hillspur wood". |

| Halsetown | HALLS'town | 1m SW St. Ives on B3311 | Built by James Halse |

Details: Halse(1769-1838) owner of St. Ives Consols Mine and MP for St. Ives, built houses for miners to secure his seat(each tenant having enough land to qualify for a vote).

Halvosso	Hal'VOSS'o (archaic Hal'VUZZA)	4m W Falmouth off A394	Summer pastures
Halzephron Cliff	Hal'ZEF'run Cliff	3.5m SW Helston off A3083	Hell cliff
Hannafore	HANNA'four	.75m S.Looe off A387	Haven way
Hannibal's Carn	Hannibal's Carn	2.5m SW Zennor off B3306	Might be named after legendary giant Holiburn.

Detail: Also suggested Hannibal Thomas, an 18C farmer from a nearby farm.

| Hantergantick | Han'ter'GAN'tek | .75m SE St. Breward off A30 | Home farm near border |

| Harlyn Bay | HAR'lin Bay | 2.5m W Padstow off B3276 | Facing the water |

Detail: Holy well of St. Cadoc .25m S of St. Cadoc Farm

Harrowbarrow	Harro'barro	2m E Callington off A390	Grey or boundary wood or Arrer'barrer
Harrowbridge	Harro Bridge	2m SE Jamaica Inn off A30	Bridge of battles
Hatt	Hat	3m NW Saltash on A388	From shape of nearby hill
Hawk's Tor	Hawkster	8m NE Bodmin off A30	Hawk's tor
Hawkstor Downs	Hawkster Downs	3m NE Blisland off A30	Hawk's tor downs

Detail: Stripple stones henge monument

| Haye | Hey | 1m W Callington off A388 | Field or enclosure |
| Hayle River | Hail River | Rising near Townshend to Hayle Estuary. The Cornish word for estuary 'heyl' was given to the whole river and place. |

Detail: There was a house called Heyl across causeway from present town.

| Hayle | Hail | on A30 | Estuary |

Details: Port of Hayle, 19C industrial development, Harvey's Foundry employed more than 1,000 people. First steam-powered road carriage built by Richard Trevithick here. Rick Rescorla from Hayle, security official at World Trade Center, New York, died in terrorist attack after saving many lives on September 11, 2001. St. Elwyn's Church 1888 by J.D. Sedding. Hayle Estuary Nature Reserve. Paradise Wildlife Park has bred choughs. Penpol Garden, famous for roses. Tourist Centre: Lethlean Lane. 01736-754399

| Hayle Copperhouse | Hail Copperhouse | in E Hayle | |

Details: Engine house near Steamer Hill, built 1834, was first steam-using railway in Cornwall carrying ore from mines near Hayle to smelting works at Redruth.

Heamoor	HAY'more	in NW Penzance off A 30	Marsh at Hea
Helford	HEL'fud	6.5m E Helston off B3293	Originally heyl-ford or estuary crossing place.
Helford Passage	HELL'fud Passidge	4.5m SW Falmouth near Mawnan Smith	Crossing place

42

Heligan	Hel'IG'un	4.5m SW St. Austell off B3273	Willow trees.

Details: Lost Garden (open to public). Manor attached to Clowance and St. Aubyns in 14C. Now Tremayne family.

Helland	HELL'und	3m N Bodmin off A30	Ancient church site

Details: Church dedicated to St. Seninan or Synnie (see Sithney), or St. Helen. Church, 13C, 15C, largely rebuilt 1883, has arcade to 15C S chapel, slate memorial early 16C.

Helland Bridge	HELL'und Bridge	3m N Bodmin off A30 by River Camel	Old place. (see previous entry)

Detail: One of best medieval bridges in county with four pointed arches. The Old Mill Herbary, Paul Jackson pottery

Hellescott	Hel'ESS'cot?	3.5m NW Launceston off B3254	Old court
Hellesveor	HELLES-veer	1m W St. Ives off B3306	Great old court
Helman Tor	Hell'man TOR	3m NW Lostwithiel off B3269	Rock outcrop, named after Helman family
Helsbury Castle	HELLS'bry? Castle	3m SW Camelford off B3266	Old court ruins

Details: Edward,the Black Prince, said to have visited deer park in 14C. Remains of hillfort castle and chapel.

Helston	HELLS'tun	on A394	Ancient court and manorial centre.

Details: Domesday - Heliston. Charter of 1201 gave borough status; Charter of Tinners in 1305 became coinage town. Grylls Monument 1834, to Humphrey Millett Grylls, public benefactor. Parish church, 1762, dedicated to St. Michael, by Thomas Edwards of Greenwich(on site of earlier church damaged in storm 1727), has brass chandelier 1762. Cornish crosses in Cross St. Holy well at Ventron Vedna 1.5m W. Market House, 1837, by W. Harris of Bristol. Chapel 1840. Methodist church 1888.Angel Hotel, part 16C, has assembly room. Bob Fitzsimmons (1863-1917), world champion at three weights, middleweight 1891, heavyweight 1896, 1897, lightheavyweight 1903, born here. Annual Flora Dance in May. Folk Museum. Flambards Theme Park. Tourist Office: 79 Meneage St. 01326-565431.

Helstone	HELL'stun	2m SW Camelford off A39	Ancient court and estate (from original spelling of Helston)

Detail: The 'e' was added later to avoid confusion with the southern town

Hendra	HEN'dra	5.5m NW St. Austell on B3279	Home farm or old farm
Hendra	HEN'dra	NW area of Truro on A39	Home farm or old farm

Detail: There are over 30 places of this name in Cornwall.

Hensbarrow Downs	HENS'burra Downs	3.5m NW St. Austell off B3274	Hind (female deer's) barrow

Detail: There is also a Cocksbarrow 1m to SW, a 19C village.

Henwood	HEN'wood	6m N Liskeard off B3254	Hens' wood
Herniss	HER'niss	3m W Penryn on A394	Long valley
Herodsfoot	HERODS'foot	3.5m SW Liskeard off A38,by West Looe River	Foot of a stream at Herod's Wood.

Detail: Church of All Saints 1850 has 14C font from St. Martin chapel, Respryn.

Heskyn	HES'kin	5.5m W Saltash off A38	Sedge
Hessenford	HESS'n'fud	4m NE Looe off A387 by River Seaton	Witches' ford

Details: Church of St. Anne 1832 by Street in lancet style, rebuilt 1871 .5m E Holy well of St. Anne.

Hewas Water	Hewers Water	4m SW St.Austell on A390	Summer grazing

Detail: The Tortoise Garden, Lower Sticker.

Hick's Mill	Hick's Mill	4m SW Truro off A39	Mill named after Hicks family
High Street	High Street	3.5m NW St. Austell off A3058	18C village high up on former downland

Detail: The settlement was at the highest point of route from St. Austell to Newquay, and may have been paved at this point.

Higher Condurrow	Higher Kn'DER'a	.5m SE Camborne off A3047	Meeting of waters
Higher Penponds	Higher Pen'PONDS	1m SW Camborne off B3303	Bridge end.

Detail: Trevithick Cottage (home of Richard Trevithick) open to public

Higher Tolcarne	Higher Tol'CARN	2.5m NW St. Columb Major off A39	Top of a rock pile
Highertown	High'ertown	In W. Truro off A390	Above the town
Hingston Down	HING'stun Down	2m NE Callington off A390	Hengest hill or stallion's hill
Holmbush	HOM'bush (archaic Umbush)	Eastern fringe of St. Austell off A390	Holly bush
Holywell Bay	HOLY'well Bay (not Holly'well!)	3.5m SW Newquay off A3075	Two holy wells, one above the dunes, one in a cave.

Detail: Originally Porth Island (cove of a little estuary). Leisure Park.

Horningtops	HORNING'tops	2.5m SE Liskeard on B3252	Hill with iron deposits.

Detail: Great Trethew Pleasure Park.

Horsebridge	Horsebridge	2.5m E Stoke Climsland linking Cornwall & Devon.	Old horse bridge

Detail: Seven arches, built 1437.

Hot Point	Hot Point	1m E Lizard off A3083	Obscure Water boiling on rocks?
Hughtown	HEW'town	SW St. Mary's Isles of Scilly	From promontory called hew (a spur of land)

Details: Old church is part of the original nave divided from a side chapel. The new church, built 1837 (instigated by William IV), has Willis organ, wooden gilded lion from Sir Cloudesley Shovel's flagship Association wrecked 1707, 16C Italian painting, cisterns on terrace 1727. Main street has late 18C & early 19C attractive granite houses.

Hugus	HEW'gus	3m W Truro off A 390	Above a wood
Hurlers	HER'lers	4.5m N Liskeard off B3254 at Minions	Three Bronze Age stone circles said to look like hurling players

I

Idless	EED'less	1.75m N Truro off B3284	Aspen trees

Detail: Holy well of St. Clare N of village (no remains as building pulled down to find legendary hoard of money).

Iland	ILL'und	4.5m SW Launceston off B3254	Obscure
Illogan	Il'LUGG'un	2m NW Redruth off A30	After St. Lugan

Details: Nothing known of the saint, except that the tomb of a saint was preserved and honoured in the late 15C. Cornish name of churchtown was Eglossalau, became English 'hallow'- church in marshes. Tower of old 14C church stands next to church built in 1846, which has Basset monuments. Holy well or parish well at Ventonraze. Famous engineer Sir Richard Tangye born in village.

Ince Castle	IN'z Castle	2m SW Saltash off A38	From enys, isolated place

Details: Brick house with four corner towers built early 17C for Henry Killigrew MP. It was captured for Parliament in Civil War. Ruin rebuilt 1920. Serious fire in 1988, house again rebuilt by Viscount & Viscountess Boyd.

Innis Downs	IN'is Downs	1m SW Lanivet off A30 Nr main roundabout	Remote spot.
Insworke	Inswork	1.5m S Torpoint off B3247	Island or isolated place
Indian Queens	Indian Queens	7m SE Newquay off A30	19C village named from inn around which it grew.

Detail: According to the experts, Pocahontas never went there. Screech Owl Sanctuary.

Isles of Scilly	Isles of Silly	Lie W of Penwith	Origins are difficult to unravel, but may be Norse or Roman.

Detail: Tourist Office: Hugh Street, Hughtown, St. Mary's. 01720-422536.

J

Jacobstow	JACOB'stow (archaic Yap'stawe)	7m S Bude off A39	Holy place of St. James.

Details: Church, 15C, restored 1887, has 87ft tower, Elizabethan altar table, pulpit of bench ends, stoup. Holy well of St. James .5m NW.

Jamaica Inn	Jamaica Inn	at Bolventor on A30 10m NE Bodmin	Was originally New Inn

Details: Renamed for Trelawny family, governors of Jamaica in 18C. Discovered by Daphne du Maurier 1930, who used the name for one of her books. Memorial room with her desk and typewriter. Mr. Potter's Museum of Curiosities.

Joppa	Shoppa?	at St. Just off A3071	Workshop

K

Kea	KEY (once pronounced Kay)	1.5m SW Truro off A39	After St. Kea

Details: Place originally Landighe, but named after St. Kei or St. Kea in 1451. He is believed to have sailed in a granite trough from Ireland, founded a community here, visited Glastonbury, & later returned from his monastery at Cleder in Brittany to make peace between King Arthur and Mordred. Parish has three churches (see entry under Old Kea). All Hallows, 3m to NW, built 1802 by James Wyatt, pulled down in 1895. Replacement by Fellowes Prynne has lead spire and steep tiled roof, Norman font of Bodmin type.

Kehelland	K'HELL'und	2m NW Camborne off A30	Grove at an ancient church site, or could be a Dark Age cemetery
Kelly Bray	Kelly BRAY	1m N Callington on A388	Grove on or near hill or dappled grove
Kelsey Head	KEL'see Head	3m W Newquay off A3075	From abandoned manor of Kelsey

Detail: Promontory fort

Kelynack	K'LIN'eck	.75m S St. Just on B3306	Holly grove

Detail: Near Land's End Aerodrome

Kenidgjack	K'NID'jick	1m NW St. Just	Place with plenty of firewood
Kennack Sands	KEN'ick Sands	2m NE Cadgwith off A3083	Marshy sands with reeds

Detail: Local pottery (including DIY)

Kennal Vale	Ken'ul Vale	2.5m NW Penryn off A393	Fertile place?

Details: Once produced gunpowder, and had 40 mills of various sorts within 5 miles. Lady Holy well .5m W of Ponsanooth.

Kennards House	Ken'uds House	2.5m W Launceston on A30	Kenna's House?
Kenneggy	K'NEG'ee	2m NW Camborne off A30	Marshes or reed beds
Kenneggy	K'NEG'ee	3m SE Marazion off A394	Marshes or reed beds
Kenwyn	KEN'win	in NW Truro off B3284	White or holy ridge?

Details: Original dedication thought to be to St. Keyne. Church, re-dedicated by Bishop Branscombe 1259 to St: Cuby, 13C,15C, restored 1820,1862,has alabaster reredos, fireplace in S. transept, lychgate with slate hung upper storey, once school. Holy well in churchyard. The church was the original mother church of Truro. Bishop's Palace (formerly the vicarage) 1780 nearby.

Kernick	KER'nick	1m SW Penryn off A39	Little nook or craggy place
Kerris	Kare'ris	2.5m SW Penzance off B3315	Fortified place?

Detail: Roundago is an ancient enclosure nearby.

Kestle Barton	KESS'l Barton	6m SE Helston off B3293	Settlement (from castel, hamlet or settlement)
Kestle Mill	KESS'l Mill	2.5m SE Newquay off A3058	From nearby farm of Kestle (originally Castel, meaning hamlet or settlement).

Detail: Trerice Elizabethan Manor. National Trust.

Keybridge	KEEbridge	4.5m N Bodmin off B3266 Between Camel and De Lank Rivers	Important bridge ?
Kilhallon	Kil'HAL'un	3m NE St. Blazey off A390	Grove of ash trees
Kilkhampton	Kilk'HAM'tun	4m NE Bude on A39	Stone circle at meadow farm

Details: Church, dedicated to St. James, built by Grenville family in 1485 on site of Norman church, restored 1860 under Sir Gilbert Scott, has fine Norman S door, wagon roof, bench ends,Royal Arms Charles ll, slate memorial 1727, memorials to Grenvilles, some by pupil of Grinling Gibbons. Holy well of St. Peter 1.5m S. Brocklands Adventure Park.

Killiganoon	Killi'g'NOON	3m SW Truro on A39	Nut tree grove
Killigarth	KILLY'garth	2.5m SW Looe off A387	Enclosure or Cat nook
Killigrew	KILL'i'groo	in central Falmouth off A39	Nut grove
Killiow	Kill'you	2m SW Truro off A39	Groves

Details: Late 18C house, with early core, converted coach house, golf range.

Killivose	Killi'VOSE	1m SW Camborne off B3303	Grove by a wall
Kilmar Tor	Kil'ma Tor	7m N Liskeard off B3254	Near Twelve Men's Moor Horse's back
King Arthur's Hall	King Arthur's Hall	2.5m NE St. Breward	Named after King Arthur

Detail: Large rectangular earth bank enclosure with 7ft high facing stones.

King Doniert's Stone	King Don'YERTS Stone	1m NW St. Cleer off B3254	Dumgarth, King of Cornwall d.875.

Detail: King Doniert's Cross. Cornwall Heritage Trust

Kingsand	KING'sand	3m S Torpoint off B3247	King's beach, after 16C King family
Kingston	KINGS'tun	3.5m N Callington off A388	Royal manor or king's farm
Kirland	KER'lund	1m S Bodmin off B3268	Enclosed site with land?

Detail: Thomas Hardy's first wife, Emma Gifford, lived in the old manor in 1860's

Kit Hill	Kit Hill	1.5m N Callington off A385	Kite's hill? (bird)

Details: Mines, quarries, burial mounds. Site given to Cornwall County Council by Prince Charles in 1985.

Kuggar	KUGG'er (to rhyme with 'rugger')	8m SE Helston off B3293	Winding stream
Kynance Cove	KY'nans Cove	1.5m NW Lizard off A3083	Ravine or gorge

Detail: National Trust nature reserve with unusual plants.

L

Ladock	LAD'uck	6m NE Truro on B3275	From St. Ladoca

Details: The saint is said to have come from Ireland with other saints. Church, consecrated in 1268, 13C, 15C, restored 1864 by Street, has wagon roof, rood screen, bench ends in lectern, William Morris and Burne-Jones stained glass windows, stocks. Holy well of St. Ladoca .5m NE.

Laity Moor	LAY'ti Moor	2m N Redruth off B3300	Milk house,dairy
Lamanva	Le'MAN'va	2m SW Penryn near Argal Reservoir	Sacred enclosure?

Detail: Military Vehicle Museum

Lamellion	Le'MELL'ee'un	in SW Liskeard off A38	Mill valley
Lamorna Cove	Le'MORN'a Cove	3m SE St.Buryan off B3315	Valley of the Mornow stream

Details: Granite quarries. Home of artist S.J. Lamorna Birch, who adopted the name to distinguish himself from another artist named Birch.

Lamorran	Le'MOR'an	4m SE Truro off A3078 near River Fal	After female patron saint St. Morenna, of whom litle known

Details: Church,mainly 13C, rebuilt 1845 and 1853, has slate memorials 1665,1666. Gothic cross in churchyard.

Lamorran House Gardens	Le'MOR'an House Gardens	Upper Castle Road, St. Mawes.	

Detail: Mediterranean Italianate garden open to public.

Lanarth	Lan'ARTH	4m NE Wadebridge off A39	Clearing
Landewednack	Lan'de'WED'nuck	near the Lizard off A3083	Church site of St. Winwaloe

Details: Cornish saint who founded Landevennec monastery. Church,14C,15C,restored 1860,has tower in serpentine, Norman S door, font with inscription, piscinas, stoup, groined porch roof, squint, old woodwork in roofs, pulpit, desk.

Landrake	Lan'DRAKE (old form 'Larrick')	3m NW Saltash off A38.	Clearing

Details: Church, dedicated to St. Michael, Norman, 15C, restored 1877, has 100ft tower, S Norman door, piscina, wagon roofs with bosses, alabaster reredos, screens 1905, squint, brass with effigy in armour 1509, slate monuments 1607.Birthplace of Robert Jeffrye, a 17C Lord Mayor of London, founder of Shoreditch almshouses, now a museum. Holy well .25m w.

Land's End	Land's End	end of A30	The end of the land (Cornish "pedn an gwlase")

Details: Exhibitions, First & Last House, hotel & restaurant. Aerodrome near St. Just.

Landulph	Lan'DULPH	2m NE Saltash off A388 by River Tamar	Deleck's church site.

Details: Deleck might have been St. Dilic (one of Broccan's children), St. Illick or French St. Dilecq. Church, patron St. Leonard, Norman, 14C, 15C,restored 1901,has 14C inner S door, niche & piscina, 15C rood screen, panelling 1600, bench ends, 17C tomb chest, brass with inscription to Theodore Palaelogus, last male descendant of Christian Emperors of Greece. Holy well .25m W.

| Lane | Lane | Southern fringe of Newquay off A392 | From lan (monastic close) or English lane. |
| Laneast | Lan'ast | 7m W Launceston off A395 | Chapel of Lanast ('Lan'church site, with personal name?) |

Details: Church dedicated to Saint Sativola (or Sidwell)who was the sister of Paul, Bishop of St. Pol de Leon. Church has some Norman remains, 14C,15C,restored 1850,has fine wagon roofs, Early English lancet window N transept, 14C W doorway,15C glass in chancel, rood screen and carved benches. Holy well SE in 16C building. Cornish Cross 1m NW. John Couch Adams, who discovered planet Neptune in 1845, born here 1819.

| Lanescot | Lan'ESS'cot | 4m NE St. Austell off A390 | Sacred land |

Detail: The Saints Way runs from here to Tywardreath

Langdon	Lang'DUN	4m NW Launceston off B3254	Long hill
Langore	Lan'GOR	2.5m NW Launceston off B3254	Valley with a stream
Lanhainsworth	Lan'HAINS'worth	1m NE St. Columb Major off A39	Friends' holy place
Lanherne	Lan'HERN	in St. Mawgan 4m NE Newquay off A3059	Holy place of St. Hernow

Details: Home to Carmelite nuns for several centuries until 2001 when Franciscan Order moved in. Good Cornish cross in garden.

| Lanhydrock | Lan'HIGH'drock | 2.5m SE Bodmin off A38 | Church site of Hydrek. |

Details: The saint was known as St. Ydrocus in 15C. Church, 15C, restored 1888, has old woodwork in porch roof, Royal Arms 1621, alabaster reredos, memorials 1599, 1689.Tall Cornish cross. Holy well W of church in garden. 17C and 19C house of Robartes family with gatehouse until 1953. Garden, grounds, shop and restaurant. National Trust. Trebyn Quoit 1.25m SW.

| Lanivet | Lan'IV'et | 3m SW Bodmin on A389 | Church site on a pagan sacred place |

Details: St. Nevet, patron saint, linked with Nevet of Lannevet in Brittany? Church, 15C restored 1864 when wall paintings destroyed, has Norman capital, probably from nearby St. Bennet priory, font with 14C panels, life-size slate monument 1632. Inscribed stones and crosses from 6C in churchyard of great interest. On Saints'Way. Lakeview Country Park 1.5m SW.

| Lanjeth | Lan'JETH | 2.5m W St. Austell off A3058 | Roebuck valley |
| Lanlivery | Lan'LIV'ry | 5m NE St. Austell off A390 | Livri's church site |

Details: Patron saint said to be either St. Brevita or St. Dunstan. Church, rebuilt 15C, restored 1878-91, has 97ft tower, wagon roofs, large 15C font, floor slab 1547, memorials 1643, 1758, 1839. Holy well of St. Bryvyth to W.

| Lanner | LAN'er | 2m SE Redruth on A393 | Clearing |

Details: Parish Church 1845, font formerly in St. Dunstan's Fleet St) with two Cornish Crosses from Chapel Hill (probably from Catholic chapel destroyed in Reformation), Wesley Methodist Church 1828,Primitive Chapel 1861, Bible Christian Chapel 1817. Rough Street, thought to date from Roman times was track used by tin traders and pilgrims between St. Michael's Mount and St. Day. Heyday during mining era in 19C.esp. Tresavean Mine, the third largest copper mine in Cornwall. Figgy Dowdy's Well at Carnmarth. On Cornish Mineral Tramway Trails.

| Lanreath | Lan'RETH | 6m SW Liskeard off B3359 | Redoc's church site. |

Details: Dedicated to St. Marnarch, and later to West Countryman St. Dunstan, who was chief counsellor to Kings of Wessex, forming coronation rites still used today.Church,Norman, 15C,tactfully restored 1887 has wagon roofs, painted rood screen, Elizabethan pulpit, bench ends, altar table, Jacobean chancel stalls, carved wood Grylls monument 1623, stocks. Court house S of church, 1610.Folk & Farm Museum. Porfell Animal Land.

Eagle House, Launceston

| Lansallos | Lan'SAL'oss | 3m E Fowey off B3359 near cliffs between Polruan & Polperro. | Salwys's church site. |

Details: Patron was St. Ildierna, a virgin, dedicated 1321. Remains of Bishop, St. Hyldren, said to be buried in church. Church 15C, restored 1884,has piece of Celtic font, Norman stones in walls, each pier of one piece of granite, carved wagon roofs, 34 benches 1490 - 1520, Jacobean wardrobe, 13C knight & lady effigy, slate coffin slab 1579. The church has been struck by lightning twice, shrapnel 1941, fire 1949 and hurricane 1990.

| Lanteglos Highway | Lan'TEG'loss Highway | 1.5m NE from ferry at Bodinnick | Church valley |

| Lanteglos by Camelford | Lan'TEG'loss by Camelford | 1.5m SW Camelford | Church valley. |

Details: Dedicated to St. Julitta, who may have been Juliana in the lists of the children of Broccan. Church, mother church to Camelford, Norman,14C,15C,restored 1872,has Norman masonry in chancel & transept,14C W doorway, sedilia, wagon roofs, niche and stoup, Elizabethan commandment boards,15C glass in S aisle windows, inlaid organ case said to have belonged to George III, pillar stone with Saxon inscription. Rectory designed by Pugin 1847. Holy well of St. Julitta 1m NE. Castle Goff .5m W of church ancient barrows. Bowood Golf Course on site of deer park.

| Lanteglos-by-Fowey | Lan'TEG'loss by Foy | 1.5m E Fowey by ferry | Church valley |

Details: Church dedicated to St. Willow, an Irishman, piloted by fish up Pont Pill, after being beheaded he picked up his head and placed it where church should be built. Church,Norman, 14C, 15C, 17C, restored 1905, has Norman work in tower arches, S door jambs, 13C font, piscina, fine 14C roof chamfered timbers N. aisle, others moulded, bench ends, pews, altar table 1634, tomb chest 1440, brass 1525. Three Cornish crosses in rectory garden.

Latchley   **LATCH'li**   2m NW Gunnislake   Wetland grove
off A390

Lanyon Quoit   **Lin'YEYN Koyt**   2m NW Madron off A3071 Cold pool
Details: Neolithic chambered tomb of three uprights with capstone.

Launcells   **LAWN'cells**   2m E Bude off A3072   Church site of Seles
Details: Church, said to be dedicated to St. Swithin though suggested it was a "cell" of the
Austin Canons at Hartland Abbey who held its jurisdiction. Rededicated in 1321 to St.
Andrew. Called "The least spoilt church in Cornwall" by John Betjeman, it is mainly 15C,
unrestored, has wagon roof, Polyphant stone S arcade,15C Barnstaple ware encaustic
tiles in chancel, wall painting of Isaac sacrifice, 60 good bench ends, box pews,wall tomb
1624, Goldsworthy Gurney, inventor, buried in churchyard. Hawker's poem "The Ringers
of Launcells Tower" commemorates George III's jubilee. Holy well S of church.

Launceston   **LAN'son**   off A30   Originally Lan-Stefan
                not LAWN'sun   (St. Stephens church
                                                site). (as found in 1478)
Details: English name Dunheved means hill end. Large church dedicated to St. Mary
Magdalene, built 1511-24 by Sir Henry Trecarrel, restored 1852, has 14C tower, stone
carved exterior, fine carved pulpit, monuments 1650, 1677, 1731. Medieval cross in
churchyard. Castle 13C.North and South Gates. Lawrence House Museum, Georgian
houses, steam rail way & museum, remains of priory, St. Thomas church, Norman, 14C,
15C, restored 1874, St. Stephen church and Holy well on hill NW above town. Tourist
Office: Market House Arcade, Market St. 01566-772321.

Lavethan   **Le'VETH'un**   4.5m E Bodmin off A30   Birch tree valley
Detail: Four Cornish crosses

Lawhitton   **Lor'WIT'un**   2m SE Launceston   Valley of Gwethen
off B3362
Details: Church dedicated to St.Michael, 13C, 15C,restored 1860, 1873, has bench ends,
pulpit 1655, slate memorial 1683,Coade stone 1796. Holy well E of church. Greystone
Bridge 1.5m SE, built 1439.

Leedstown   **LEEDS'tun**   4m SW Camborne   Created by Duke of
                                on B3280   Leeds in 1867, whose
                                                  family married into the
                                                      Godolphins.
Detail: Birthplace of famous cosmetics producer Elizabeth Arden.

Lelant   **Le'LANT**   3m SE St. Ives on A3074   Anta's church site
Details: The saint had a chapel on rocks at entrance to Hayle River. Church, later dedicated
to St. Uny, an Irish missionary who landed in Hayle, Norman,13C, 15C, restored 1873, has
Norman N arcade, S door spandrels, stoup, slate memorials 1620, 1635, 1698, 18C copper
sundial over porch. Five Cornish crosses in churchyard, cemetery & nearby. Holy Well of St.
Uny .5m SE; Holy well of Fenton Sauras 1.25m SE at Tredreath.

Lerryn   **Le(short'e')rin**   3m SE Lostwithiel   Waters or flood
off A390
Details: Two 16C bridges of two arches and low tide stepping stones.

Lesnewth   **Lis'NEWTH**   2m E Boscastle off A39   New court or
                                                         administrative centre
Details: Church of St. Michael (originally St. Kneut) rebuilt 1866,has Norman columns
chancel, altar stone with 5 crosses as window base, piscina, tombstone 1680. Cornish
cross, with head used as pigs' trough. Holy well of St. Austen on Hendra Farm.

Levant Mine   **Le'VANT Mine**   1m NW Pendeen off B3306 Named after St. Levan ?
Detail: Beam engine driven by steam. National Trust

Lewannick   **L'WONN'ick**   5m SW Launceston   Church site of Gwenek
off A30   or Gwenoc.
Details: Dedicated to St. Martin (see entry under St. Martin by Looe) Church rebuilt 15C
and after 1890 fire, W door richly decorated, wagon roof in porch, two inscribed stones and
cresset stone with seven cups Three holy wells W, NW, NE. Three Cornish crosses in area.

Ley   **Lay**   5.5m NW Liskeard   Ley field or flat stone
off A38

50

Webb's Hotel at Liskeard

| Lezant | Le'ZANT | 3.5m S Launceston off A388 | Sant's church site. |

Details: Sant was the father of St. David. Patron saints St. Briochus & St. Michael rededicated 1259. Church, 14C, 15C, restored 1869, has some Norman work, piscinas, aumbry, wagon roofs, slate altar tomb to Trefusis (family of Flushing), Henry Trecarrell buried near organ, stone cross in S porch. Two Holy wells, St. Michael N of church; St. Lawrence .75m N near clapper bridge.

| Ligger Point | LIGG'a Point | 4m SW Newquay off A3075 | Seaweed or cliff. |

Detail: Also known as Perran Bay from patron saint of parish.

| Linkinhorne | Link'in'HORN (some say LINK'in'horn, others LINK'in'HORN!) | 3.5m NW Callington off B3257 | Kenhoarn's church site. |

Details: Patron St.Mylor was believed to be Breton abbot-bishop, St. Meloir (see entry under Mylor),but also claimed he was the son of the Duke of Cornwall, whose hand and foot were chopped off when a child and replaced with silver ones. He was martyred in 411. Church,15C,16C, restored 1891, has Tower(120ft) rebuilt 16C by Sir Henry Trecarrel, wagon roof, 15C wall paintings, 13c font, altar slab, bench ends, grave stones by Daniel Gumb. Holy well of St. Melor .5m S, where gold beaker found.

| Liskeard | Liss'KARD | on A390 off A38 | Kerwyd's court or stags court. |

Details: Church, dedicated to St. Martin, second largest in Cornwall,Norman,15C,restored 1793,1878, 1890 has Norman W door & windows, unusual chancel chapels, piscinas, pulpit 1636, 13 consecration crosses on outer walls, new tower 1903. R.C. Church Our Lady & St.Neot 1863, Stuart House 17C,Museum,Pipe Well, Lady Park Well 1.5m W. Looe Valley railway. Moorswater Viaduct to W. built 1881. Information: Foresters Hall, Pike Street. 01579-349148

Little Petherick   Little PETH'er'ick 2m SW Padstow on A389   Dedicated to St. Petroc
Details: Called "Little" as opposed to Padstow, also dedicated to St. Petroc). The saint is
supposed to have spent much of his time up to his neck in the local river reciting the
psalter. Church,14C,18C, rebuilt 1858 by William White, restored 1908 by Comper, is
lately Anglo-Catholic, has arch from ruined church of St.Constantine,13C Purbeck marble
memorial slab,15C font, screen with gilded Seraphims of six wings, Molesworth family
patrons, N chapel built 1916 to Hon. Mrs Riley(nee Molesworth).

Lizard   LIZ'ud   10m SE Helston on A3083   High place, or name
          (previously Les'ARD)   given by chartmakers
                                                    from likeness to a
                                                    lizard's tail.
Details: Lighthouse 1752. Most southerly place in England.

Lizard Church   LIZ'ud Church   .5m E of Lizard (see Landewednack church)
Cove   Cove
Lockengate Moor Lock'n'GATE More 6m NE St. Austell off A391   Turnpike locking gate
Loe Pool   Low Pool   2m SW Helston off B3304   Tidal pool
Details: Largest natural freshwater lake in Cornwall, famous for wintering wildfowl. Penrose
House 17C & later

Loe Beach   Low Beach   S of Feock   Creek or tidal pool
Logan Rock   LOG'un Rock   2.5m SW St. Buryan   Rocking stone, from
                               off B3315   dialect "logging" to
                                                      rock
Details: Was rocked off perch in 1824 by Lt. Goldsmith and revenue cutter crew, replaced
and now moves with difficulty.

Loggans Moor   LUG'uns Moor   NE fringe of Hayle   From personal name?
                                   off A30/B3301
London Apprentice London Apprentice 2m S St. Austell off B3273   Named after young
                                                                      men who came to find
                                                                      work in local mines
Long Cross   Long Cross   SW Port Isaac off B3314   Victorian gardens
Longdowns   LONG'downs   2.5m SW Penryn   19C village on former
                               on A3941   downland
Longlands   LONG'lands   2m W Tamar Bridge   Large fields ?
                               off A38
Longrock   Long Rock   2m E Penzance off A30   From the Long Rock
Detail: Rock in sea south of Longrock, exposed at low tide.

Longships   LONG'ships   1.5m W.Land's End   Rocks which resemble a
                 (Carn Bras)   string of vessels.
Detail: Light house built 1873 by William Douglas is 117ft high.

Looe Island   Loo Island   1m S Looe   Monks' church site
Detail: St. Michael of Lammana 13C.

Looe   Loo   on A387   Estuary
Details: Until 16C the name usually meant East Looe. S.E. Cornwall Discovery Centre,
early buildings, museums, fishing, monkey sanctuary. Information: The Guildhall, Fore
St. 01503-262072 (see also East Looe and West Looe)

Looe Mills   Loo MILLS   1.5m NW Liskeard off A38   Mills on river
Lostwithiel   Los'WITH'i'el   10m SW Liskeard on A390   Tail of a wooded area
                                                              called Withiel.
Details: Capital of Cornwall in 13C. Also seat of Duchy Parliament with Stannary Court &
Hall of the Exchequer. Civil War battle of 1644 nearby, with troops garrisoned in church.
St. Bartholomew Church, 14C, restored 1890, has broach spire with dormer windows, the
tower being built over a public right of way (closed 1878), clerestory, good E window,
remarkable 14C font, piscine, standing figure alms box. Lantern cross in churchyard.
Stannnary Court, Guildhall, Old Grammar School, 14C bridge of five arches. Museum,
Fore St. Information: At Community Centre. 01208-872207

Lowertown   LOWER'town   1m N Helston off B3297   Village in hill bottom

Lower Tregantle Lower Tr'GAN'tl 3m SW Torpoint off B3247 Silvery stream
Detail: Tregantle Fort,19C coastal defence.

Luckett   **LUCK'it**   3m NE Callington   Leofa's cottage
                                          off B3257
Detail: Called Lovecott in 1557

Ludgvan   **LUDG'van**   3.5m NE Penzance on B3309 Place of ashes (near
                     (generally) **LUD'jin** or **LID'jin** (locally)   ancient burial site).
Details: Church, dedicated to St. Lewdegran (carving over porch),re-dedicated to St. Paul 1336,is 14C,15C, restored 1914, has unusual Norman font, wall painting found 1740, memorials to historian Dr. Borlase and family of Humphry Davy. Two Cornish crosses in churchyard. Holy well N of church also Holy well of Collurian.

Lusty Glaze   **LUSTY Glayse**   in NE Newquay off A3058 Grey/green
                                                                  promontory
Luxulyan   **Lux'ZILL'yen**   4m NE St. Austell   Sulyan's chapel.
                                          off A390
Details: Church, originally dedicated to St. Sulian (or Julian), a Welsh saint who went to Brittany. In 1412 dedication changed to Cyriac & Julitta (popular cult saints in time of Crusaders), 15C, restored 1883, has wagon roofs, groined porch roof, piscina, memorial to architect Sylvanus Trevail. Cornish cross in churchyard. Holy well of St. Cyr near village pump. Nearby quarries provided porphry for Wellington's tomb in St. Paul's Cathedral.

Lynher River   **LIE'ner** (old **LIN'er**) Starts on Bodmin Moor,   Obscure - flowing river?
comes down through Rilla Mill, Newbridge and Notter Bridge, joins Tamar at Saltash

M

Mabe   **MAYB**   2m S Penryn off   Mabe's church site
                     (not May be!)   A39 or A394
Details: The church is dedicated to St. Laud, 6C Norman bishop, formerly a chapel of Mylor. Church, on own, 15C, rebuilt 1869 after lightning damage, has fine S.porch and W. tower door, piscina, fragments of 15C alabaster altar in reredos. Cornish cross in vicarage garden.

Mabe Burnthouse **MAYB Burnt'ouse** 1m W Penryn off A39 or A394   Burning house
                                                                            or kiln
Maders   **MAY'dus**   1.5m NW Callington off A388   Middle of moor
Madron   **MAD'run**   1.5m NW Penzance off A30   From St. Madern.
                     or **MAD'ern**
Details: Saint thought to be Welsh St. Mactronus, who founded abbey at Treguier, Brittany. Mother church of Penzance, 14C, 15C, restored 1887, has 14C sedilia & piscina, rood screen, bench ends,Jacobean tower screen, 18C altar rails,Greek Mausoleum 1820 in churchyard. Ruins of 14C Baptistery, St. Madron's Well, where rags are tied to bushes and cripples cured. Men Scryfa Down 3m NW pillar stone 5C or 6C 8ft tall with Roman inscription.

Maenporth   **MAIN'porth**   2m SW Falmouth   Stone cove
Maidenwell   **MADE'n'well**   5.5m NE Bodmin off A30 The maidens' spring
Magor   **MAY'ger**   2m NW Camborne off A30 Ruin
Detail: Site of Roman villa

Maker   **Make'r**   2.5m S Torpoint off B3247 Ruin
Detail: Church, dedicated to St. Mary & St. Julian, the Hospitaller, is isolated, mainly 15C, restored 1874, has tower used as signal station in 18C & 19C (signalman murdered in it 1763), 19C, wagon roofs & bosses,chancel bay with carving, Edgcumbe monuments. Holy well & 14C chapel of St. Julian N. Fort Picklecombe 1860.

Malpas   **Mal'pus**   1.5m SE Truro off A390 Le mal pas (Fr) - 'bad
                     or **MO'pus**   step' or difficult crossing
Details: Glastonbury Well at Sunny Corner, once a resort for many medical disorders.

Manaccan	M'NACK'un	7m SE Helston off B3293	Minster or endowed church, place of monks.

Details: Dedicated to St. Manacca, said to be associated with Archbishop Dunstan. Church, Norman, 13C, 14C, 15C, restored 1888, has Norman S door, top of Norman shaft S transept, W door has drip mould with label stop heads, piscina, squint, at one time fig tree grew out of side of nave. Holy well of Tregonnel .75m S - nearby was found feruginous sand, the source of titanium, called Manaccanite (see entry under Cornelly).

Manacles	Manacles	.75m off Manacle Point, 1.5m E of St. Keverne off B3293	Church rocks

Detail: The 'church' is perhaps a reference to spire of St. Keverne church as a landmark from the sea

Manhay	Men'HAY	2.5m NE Helston on A394	Sanctuary
Marazanvose	MARRA'zan'VOZE	4m NW Truro on A30	Market with a wall or dyke
Marazion	Marra'ZI'un	3m E Penzance off A394	Little market.

Details: The alternative name of the town was Market Jew (Thursday market), which was a separate place next to Marazion. The two places were merged in 16C - the name 'Market Jew' being commemorated in Penzance's main street. Town Charter 1257. All Saints Church 1861 by J.P.St. Aubyn replaced medieval Chapel of St. Hermes, rebuilt 1735. Memorial window to architect 1895. Methodist Chapel 1862, classical galleried. Museum. Aquarium.

Marhamchurch	MARAM'church	1.5m SE Bude off A39	Church of Morwenna

Details: She is said to be one of the children of Broccan. Also suggested she might be the English St. Merwenn, 10C abbess of Romsey. Cecilia Moys, a hermit or anchoress, lived by church, remains of her cell is in upper part of W wall. Church, 15C, restored 1840 - 1907, has Norman masonry in S transept & base of shaft, wagon roofs, piscina, aumbry, 17C pulpit, cresset stone, 17C slate memorials. Revel on Aug 12.

Markwell	MARK'well	1.5m SW Landrake off A38	Well of Aelmarch

Detail: Situated just before Markwell Farm

Marshgate	MARSH'gate	6m NE Camelford off A39	Gate leading to marsh
Mawgan-in-Meneage	MOR'gn in M'NEEG or M'NAYG	3.5m SE Helston off B3293	From patron saint of the church, St. Maugan

Details: The saint was a Welsh missionary bishop, also known in Brittany.

Mawgan-in-Pydar	MOR'gn in PY'der	4m NE Newquay off A3059	from St. Maugan (see above).

Detail: Pydar was the fourth of the nine Cornish Hundreds. (See entry under St. Mawgan).

Mawgan Porth	MOR'gn Pawth	4m NE Newquay on B3276	Cove of Maugan (originally Porth Gluvian).
Mawla	MOR'la	2m N Redruth off A30	Possibly bare place
Mawnan	MORE'nun	3m SW Falmouth amongst trees overlooking Helford river	Named after patron saint, St. Maunan, of whom little known

Details: Church, which also has patron St. Stephen (first martyr of Christian Church), 14C, 15C, restored 1684,1830,1855,1880, has lancet chancel window, 14C windows N aisle, 13C piscina,13C stone coffin lid, rood screen panels, Cornish cross head in W wall N aisle. Holy Well in garden of old rectory.

Mawnan Smith	MORE'nun Smith	3.5m SW Falmouth	Named after St. Maunan (see entry above), the "Smith" probably from smithy.
Maxworthy	MAX'worthy	5m NW Launceston off B3254	Roman derivation from Latin personal name Maximius?
Meledor	Mel'a'DER	5m NW St. Austell off A3058	Cliff
Mellangoose	Melon'GOOS	1.5m SE Helston off A394	Woodland mill

Mellangoose	Melon'GOOS	1m NW Helston off A394	Woodland mill
Mellingey	M'LINJ'ee	4.5m SE Wadebridge off A389	Mill house
Menabilly	Men'a'BILLY	5m SE St. Austell off A3082	Hill side pebbly place where colts drink

Details: Cornish Cross, wheel type.

| Menacuddle | Men'a'CUD'le | Northern fringe of St. Austell | Thicket on hillside. |

Detail: Holy well, thought to be to St.Guidel, whose chapel once adjoined the well.

| Men-An-Tol | Men'an'TOLL | 4m NW Penzance off B3306 | Stone with a hole |

Details: Megalithic holed stone (giving restricted access to burial vault). North is Men Scryfa inscribed stone

| Meneage | M'NEEGE or M'NAYGE | (district of five parishes - St. Keverne St. Mawgan, St. Martin, Manaccan and St. Anthony). | Monastic land |

Detail: May refer to several Celtic monasteries in district

| Menheniot | Mn'HEN'yut | 2.5m SE Liskeard off A38 | Possibly Hynyed/ Heniot's land or fertile place. |

Details: Church, dedicated to St. Lalluwy or Ladislas (virtuous King of Hungary in 11C) and St. Antoninus, rebuilt 1450, restored 1925, has spire, good ceiled wagon roofs with wall plates, piscina, sedilia, floor brass 1386, slate tomb 1674, bust 1726, slab 1724. Holy well on outside wall of vicarage.

Menherion	Men'HE're'un	3.5m S Redruth	Long or standing stones
Merrose	Me'rose (e as in wreck)	Northern fringe of Camborne off A30	Middle of the heath
Merry Maidens	Merry Maidens	2m SE St. Buryan off B3315	Dance of the stone maidens (maidens from 'men' meaning stone)

Detail: 19C name for stone circle of 19 stones. NE are The Pipers, said to be the musicians for the maidens, all turned to stone for dancing on the Sabbath.

| Merrymeet | MERRY'meet | 2m NE Liskeard off A390 | Pleasant meeting place, also common name for the meeting of roads |
| Merther | MUR'thur | 2.25m E Truro above Tresillian River off A3078 | Place with saint's relics |

Detail: Thought to be St. Coan, believed to have been murdered here. Eglos merther (churchtown farm nearby). Church, now disused, originally Norman, 14C, clumsily restored 1844. Holy well and chapel of St. Coan formerly existed.

| Merther Uny | Mer'ther YEW'ni | 3m NE Helston off A394 | Place with saint's relics |

Details: Dedicated to St. Uny, Irish missionary, brother of Sts. Ia and Erc, who landed at Hayle estuary led by St. Gwinear. An ancient church once existed here. Holy well of Merther Uny nearby.

Metherell	METH'rul	3m E Callington off A390	Middle hill
Methrose	METH'rose	3m NE St. Austell off A390	Place in the middle of a hill
Mevagissey	Mevva'GIZZ'ee	4.5m S St. Austell on B3273	From Saints Meva and Issey.

Details: Originally Porthilly (saltwater cove). Church of St. Peter, 15C, restored 1888, has tower with 19C saddle-back roof, piscina, Decorated window,17C memorials. Brass Well at Treleven Farm N of town. Picturesque fishing port. Some Georgian buildings. Aquarium, Model railway, Town Museum, 14 Church St. Information: St. Georges Square. 01726 - 844857.

Michaelstow	**Michaelstow**	3.5m SW Camelford off B3266	St. Michael's holy place

Details: Church, 15C, restored 1868 - 88, has piscina, original wagon roofs, benches, traces of anchorite's cell N side, slate memorials 16C, 17C. Tall Cornish cross in churchyard. Holy well of Michaelstow S of church. Holy well of Fentonadle .5m SE. Helsbury Castle, Iron Age hill fort nearby.

Middle Taphouse	**Middle Taphouse**	5m W Liskeard on A390	Alehouse
Millandreath	**Mil'an'DRETH**	1m E Looe off B3253	Mill by beach
Millbrook	**MILL'brook**	2m S Torpoint off B3247	Brook by a mill (site of mill not known).

Details: Ruined chapel of former Inswork Manor to N. Remains of industrial buildings.

Millpool	**MILL'pool**	4m NE Bodmin off A30	Mill pool
Millpool	**MILL'pool**	7m E Penzance off B3280	Mill pool
Milltown	**MILL'town**	1.5m S Lostwithiel off B3269	Mills place
Milltown	**MILL'town**	3m NE Bodmin off A30	Mills place
Minack	**MIN'ack** (to rhyme with 'tin')	3m SW St. Buryan off B3315	Stony or rocky place.

Details: Open Air Theatre built by Rowena Cade, began 1932 with Billy Rawlings and Charles Thomas Angove performing in "The Tempest". Exhibition Centre. Tel: 017736 - 810181

Mingoose	**Min'GOOZ**	1m SW St. Agnes off B3277	Edge of the wood
Minions	**MIN'yuns**	4.5m N Liskeard off B3254	Named from tumulus called Minions Mound

Details: The village was earlier called Cheesewring Railway from a local quarry railway. Nearby is The Cheesewring, The Hurlers stone circle, Stowe's Pound, Caradon & Phoenix Mines and Heritage centre.

Minster	**MIN'ster**	.75m SE Boscastle off B3266 below road	Endowed church

Details: Dedicated to St. Materiana (also Tintagel Church on cliff top), wife of a Welsh king. Mother church of Boscastle, originally a priory of Benedictine monks. Church, 15C, restored 1869 - 71, has 13C chancel window interesting 17C monuments. Holy well of St. Materiana N of church tower

Mitchell	**MIT'chul**	7m NE Truro off A30	Maid's hollow

Details: La Medeshole in 1284 may be a corruption of Lan Mehal (St. Michael's Church).

Mithian	**MITH'ee'un**	2.5m SE St. Agnes off B3277	'The pasturage' suggested

Details: Church of St. Peter built 1861 by William White was meant to serve both Mithian and Blackwater, but now isolated. Spire removed 1891, tower erected 1928. Holy well 1m N of church.

Mixtow	**MIX'toe**	1m NE Fowey off A390 (on River Fowey)	Not known

Note: Old English term for midden (dunghill) is mixen.

Moditonham	**MUD'it'un'ham**	1.5m N Saltash off A388	Not known, but OE 'Mod' means 'meeting place'
Molingey	**M'LIN'jee**	2m SW St. Austell off B3273	Mill house
Molinnis	**Mol'INN'is**	4.5m N St. Austell off A391	Bare isolated place
Mongleath	**Mon'GLEETH**	Western fringe of Falmouth	Quarry or mine
Monks Cross	**Monks Cross**	2m NE Callington on B3257	Cross roads
Moorswater	**MOORS'water**	1m W Liskeard off A38	Between moors and East Looe River

Sir John Opie's birthplace at Trevellas, Mithian, near St.Agnes.

The son of a miner, the portrait painter, who became known as "The Cornish Wonder", was discovered by the local doctor and satirist John Wolcot. All London flocked to his studio, and he became a star of the Royal Academy, painting about 750 major works in his lifetime.

| Mornick | MOR'nick | 3m NW Callington off B3257 | Ants place |
| Morvah | MOR'va | 3m NE St. Just on B3306 | Sea grave, with unknown saint buried there. |

Details: Church, dedicated to St. Bridget of Sweden who founded an order of nuns, is daughter church to Madron, was built by Knights of St. John of Jerusalem in 14C, re-dedicated 1409, but only tower remains. Rebuilt 1828. Holy well of Tregaminion, with few stones from former chapel, .5m N of church. Chun Quoit.

| Morval | MAW'vl | 2m N Looe off A387 | Obscure place name - connected with the sea? Marsh valley suggested, or St. Wenna in Morvelle |

Details: St. Wenna was one of the daughters of Broccan. Church, 15C, 16C, original N aisle roof, slate memorial 1637 to Walter Coode. Morval House nearby is E-shaped Tudor, with later additions.

| Morwenstow | MOR'wen'sto | 7m N Bude off A39 | St. Morwenna's holy place. |

Details: The saint, one of the children of Broccan, was believed to have helped build the church by carrying stone for font from the shore on her head. Church, dedicated to St. John, Norman, 13C, 15C, 17C, has Norman door, piers, arches, rood screen, bench ends, wall painting of St. Morwenna. The Rev. Robert Stephen Hawker was vicar in mid 19C, founding the Harvest Festival and writing hymns and poems. Vicarage, built by Hawker, has chimneys shaped like towers of churches he served in. Holy well of St. John and holy well of St. Morwenna (on coast). Killarney Springs Adventure & Leisure Park.

Mount	Mount	5m E Bodmin off A38	19C hamlet on former downland near farm named Mount Pleasant
Mount	Mount	4m SW Newquay off A3075	Hill village halfway up long hill
Mount Ambrose	Mount AM'brose	in Northern fringe of Redruth	Pleasant place.
Mount Edgcumbe	Mount EDGEcum	2m SE Torpoint off B3247	From Edgcumbe family

Details: Family name came from hamlet of Edgcumbe over the Tamar. House, built 1554, burnt in Second World War, rebuilt 1960. House, country park and formal gardens open to public. Holy well of St. Leonard .25m W of church.

Mount Hawke	Mount HAWKE	3.5m NE Redruth off A30/B3277	Named from local family of Hawkes in 18C. Mining village.
Mountjoy	Mount'JOY	3.5m SE Newquay on A392	House of stone
Mount Pleasant	Mount Pleasant	at St. Breward	Pleasant place
Mount Pleasant	Mount Pleasant	5m SW Bodmin off A30	Pleasant place
Mount's Bay	Mownt's Bay	off Penzance on A394	Named from St. Michael's Mount
Mousehole	Mowz'le (to rhyme with tousle)	2.5m S Penzance off B3315	After sea cave shape

Details: The harbour was originally Porth Ennis from offshore St. Clement's Isle. 16C pillared manor house.

| Muchlarnick | Much'LARN'ick | 3m NW Looe off B3359 | Glade or clearing |

Details: Divided into "Great" and "Little" in Middle Ages. Today there is North Muchlarnich and West Muchlarnick, as well as Muchlarnick itself.

| Mulfra Quoit | MULL'frer Quoit | 5m SW St. Ives off B3206 | Bare or domed hill |

Mullion	MULL'yun	5.5m S Helston off A3083 on B3359	From Breton patron saint of church St. Mollien

Details: He was later superceded by St. Melaine, named from the 6C bishop of Rennes (See entry for St. Mellion). Church, 15C, restored 1878 - 83, has early N door, 13C font, good carved bench ends, original ceiled wagon roofs, rood screen. Charles II arms, small door for dogs in S. door.

Mullion Cove	MULL'yun Cove	6.5m SW Helston off A3083 on B3359	Originally Porth Mellin, fishing cove with mill or "St. Melan's Cove".
Mylor Churchtown	MY'ler Churchtown	2m NE Falmouth off A39	From St. Meloir

Details: Early Breton abbot-bishop, not to be confused with St. Melor at Amesbury, Wiltshire, about whom there are many tales but little reliable facts(see entry for Linkinhorne).Lovely position by creek. Church, Norman, 15C, has turret on W. gable and 17C belfry, two Norman door ways, 13C font, piscina,Elizabethan pulpit, rood screen, monuments 1680,1805. Tallest Cornish cross in Cornwall at 17ft 6ins.Holy well in churchyard.

Mylor Bridge	MY'ler Bridge	2m NE Falmouth off A39 (see above entry)

Detail: The village used to be called Penoweth (new bridge).

N
Nampara	Nam'PARa	Southern fringe of Perranporth on B32384	Valley of bread

Detail: Also name of the Poldark farmhouse in Winston Graham's "Poldark"

Nancarrow	Nan'CA'row	.75m SE St. Michael Penkevil, 3.5m SE Truro off A390	Stag valley
Nancegollan	Nancy'GOLL'un	3m NW Helston on B3303	Whet stone valley
Nancekuke	Nans'KEWK	3m NW Redruth off B3300	Creek or hollow valley
Nancemelling	Nans'MELL'in	3m NW Camborne off A30	Mill valley
Nancledra	Nan'CLED'ra (or KLED'ri)	4m NE Penzance on B3311	Clodri's valley
Nanjizal	Nan'JIZ 'l	3m NE Penzance at Crowlas off A30	Low valley
Nanpean	Nan'PEA'un (archaic:Nan'PEEN)	4m NW St. Austell on B3279	Little valley

Detail: Holy well of St. Bernard now built over, was opposite gates of Nanpean Mission Church and between C & D bays of China Clays Drinnick Depot. Water still runs under concrete base and out other side. (See entry in J. Meyrick's book).

Nansavallen	Nans'a'VAL'en	1m SW Truro off A390	Apple tree or orchard valley
Nansladron	Nans'LAD'run	3m S St. Austell off B3273	Valley of thieves or holy place of St. Hadron.
Nansloe	Nans'LO	Southern fringe of Helston off A394	Valley of the sea lake, loe or pool
Nanstallon	Nan'STAl'un	1.5m W Bodmin off A389	Church site of Tallan or Valley of the River Allen (formerly River Camel)

Detail: Oak Lodge woodland garden and nursery.

Nanswhyden	Nan'SWEE'dun	3m E Newquay off A3059	White valley or valley of trees
Nare Head	Nair Head	8m SE Truro off A3078	High place or headland (from farm called Pennare)
Narkurs	NAR'kers	8m SW Torpoint off A374	Not known

Navax Point	Nay'vax Point?	4.5m NW Camborne off B3301	Summerlands

Detail: From The Knavocks grazing land nearby?

Newbridge	Newbridge	1.5m SW Callington on A390 (River Lynher)	New bridge over water

Detail: Late 15C bridge, widened and rebuilt in 1874 and 1898

New Bridge	Newbridge	in N Gunnislake on A390	New bridge over Tamar between Cornwall & Devon
Newbridge	NEW'bridge	3m NW Penzance on A3071	Name given after road bridge built over Newlyn River (formerly hale an tegan - the pretty marsh.)
Newbridge	NEW'bridge	1.5m W Truro off A390	New bridge over river
New Grimsby	New Grimsby	NW Tresco Isles of Scilly	Odin's water
Newham	NEW'um	1.75m NW Helston off A394	Farm settlement (ham - Saxon for farm)
Newham	NEW'um	Southern fringe of Truro off A390	Farm settlement (ham - Saxon for farm).

Detail: Ancient manor

Newlyn	NEW'lin	.5m S Penzance on B3315	Fleet pool

Details: Fishing port, piers built 1478, 1887, 1888, 1980. Town burnt by Spanish 1595. In 1883 had finest fleet of 100 mackerel & pilchard drivers in world. Newlyn riots of 1896 over Sunday fishing put down by militia. Pilchard works from 1851 at Tolcarne. Ship Institute 1911. New fish market 1988. Newlyn Fish Festival August. Penlee Lifeboat disaster(all crew lost 1981). Newlyn Society of Artists 1895. Newlyn Art Industries. Memorial to William Lovett, 1800 - 1877, Chartist leader. Manors of 17C & 18C. Church of St. Peter, rebuilt 1865 and 1886, has work by Ernest Proctor of Newlyn School. Penlee Quarry nearby.

Newlyn East	NEW'lin East	3.5m S Newquay off A30	From patron St. Newlina.

Details: 'East' was added after 1888 to distinguish from Newlyn near Penzance. The saint was said to be an Irish princess, who landed at Holywell Bay & went to Newlyn, where she struck her staff in the ground from which grew a fig tree. On refusing a betrothal, she was beheaded. Another story says St. Noluen crossed the sea from Britain on a leaf and was martyred near Pontivy. Church, Norman, 13C, 14C and 15C, restored 1883, has Norman masonry, 13C double piscina, 14C chancel aisle & N. doorway, screen, bench ends, royal arms, lantern cross head, Arundell monument 1691. Holy well of St.Newlina or Guron .25m from church. At Cargoll .75m from church, a 15C tithe barn with one of the best timber roofs visible in Cornwall (Pevsner). Lappa Valley Steam Railway.

Newmill	NEW'mill	2.5m NW Penzance off B3311	Place with new mill
New Mill	NEW Mill	1.5m NW Truro off B3284	Place with new mill
New Mills	NEW Mills	6.5m NE Truro on B3275	Originally Melynewyth (new mill) but dates back to 14C.
Newquay	NEW'quay	off A392	From first quay 1440

Details: Was Towan Blistra (Tewynplustri - sand dunes by ships cove?). Church of St. Michael, 1911 by Ninian Comper, restored end 20C after fire, large with Polyphant arcades, rood screen, 18C style organ. Huer's Hut with tower (for sighting pilchard shoals), Headland Hotel by Sylvanus Trevail, Wesley Methodist Church 1904.Bronze Age cliff castle and barrows. Surfing. Aquarium.Zoo. Leisure Park. Waterworld. Old Cornwall Gallery. Tourist Office: Municipal Offices, Marcus Hill 01637 - 854020

Newton Ferrers	NEW'tun Ferrers	2.5m SW Callington off A390	New settlement near Freers Farm

Details: Devon counterpart means new farm whose manor came to be held by William de Ferrers in 13C. Mansion built 1695 for Sir William Coryton. Earliest Cornish mansion of classical design without trace of Tudor survivals (Pevsner), gutted by fire 1940, some rebuilding. Clapper bridge to SE.

Sir William Golding's birthplace in Newquay.

This house in Mount Wise, Newquay, belonging to his grandmother, was where William Golding was born in 1911,and later spent many holidays. His well known book "Lord of The Flies" was published in 1954, and he was awarded the Nobel Prize for Literature in 1983. He died near Truro in 1993.

Newtown	NEW'tun	7m NW Callington off B3257	New dwellings
Newton	NEW'tun	1m NW Fowey off B3269	New dwellings
Newtown in St. Martin	NEW'tun in St. Martin	6m SE Helston off B3293	New hamlet in 19C
Nine Maidens	Nine Maidens	1.5m S Four Lanes off B3297	Maidens from 'men' meaning stones

Detail: Two circles of standing stones.

Nine Maidens	Nine Maidens	4.5m SW Wadebridge just off A39	Maidens from 'men' meaning stones

Detail: Row of standing stones

Nine Maidens	Nine Maidens	.5m NE St. Just off B3306	From stone circle, maiden from 'men' meaning stone.
Ninnesbridge	Nin'izbridge	2.75m S St. Ives off B3311	Isolated place
Noon Billas	Noon Pillas	3m SW St. Ives off B3311	Downs of naked or extinct oats

Detail: Pylas (naked oats) was the most common crop name found in fields in Penwith, (name now believed extinct).

North Cliffs	North Cliffs	2.5m NW Camborne on B3301	Cliffs on north coast
North Country	North Country	1m N Redruth off A30	Place north of Redruth
North Darley	North DAR'li	6m NW Callington on B3254	Oak wood
North Hill	North HILL	7m SW Launceston off B3254	North hindle in 1260 (hinds'wood)

Details: Large church, dedicated to St. Terney (see also St. Erney),15C restored 1870, has 14C chancel, ogee niches, ceiled wagon roofs, squint, stoup, slate table tomb with kneeling effigies 1606. Holy well of St. Torney .50m S.

North Petherwin	North PETHA'win	4.5m NW Launceston off B3254	From patron saint St. Padern, plus gwyyn' meaning blessed.

Details: The Welsh abbot-bishop was known as 'Blessed Padern', but it is possible that the saint was Peternus, a local chieftain, father of St. Constantine. (See South Petherwin). Church, Norman,14C,15C,16C, restored 1876, has Norman piers N side, old roofs, 16C ironwork S door, communion rails 1685, screens,slate memorials 1643,1638. Holy well of St. Paternus .75m W. Tamar Otter Park nearby.

North Tamerton	North TAM'er'tun	8.5m N Launceston off B3254	Estate (tun) on River Tamar

Details: Patron saint, St. Denis. Church,15C,restored 1875,has piscina, bench ends, chancel stall carvings, brass 1576,slate slab of 1706. Holy well of St. Dennis above rectory.

O

Old Kea	Old Key (old pronunication Kay)	2.5m S Truro off A39 on Truro River	From St. Kea (see entry under Kea).

Details: Only tower remains of original 15C church. Small mission church built 1863. Shaft of Cornish cross near church. New church 3 miles away to NW, All Hallows.

Otterham	OTTER'um	5.5m NE Camelford off A39	River meadow or enclosed land on River

Details: Church,dedicated to St.Dennis,drastically restored 1890, has old font base and bowls, piscina, slate memorial 1652, two medieval bells and another, chimed by churchwarden, one in each hand, the other with a foot.

Otterham Station	OTTER'um Station	4.5m NE Camelford on A39	River meadow or enclosed land on River Ottery with redundant railway station
Ottery River	OTT'ry River	Rises SE Otterham Station	Otter river

P

| Padstow | PAD'sto (archaic Padsta) | 5m NW Wadebridge end of A389 off A39 | St. Petroc's holy place. |

Details: The Welsh princely saint, said to have arrived on an altar stone, founded a monastery and struck a spring from a rock. His relics are in Bodmin church. Church, 13C, 14C, 15C, has wagon roofs, piscina, 15C font, bench ends,16C pulpit, brass 1421, effigies of Nicholas Prideaux & family 1627, 18C churchyard gates. Cornish crosses in churchyard and at Prideaux Place. Various wells in and around Padstow include Holy well of Fenton Luna SE Prideaux Place, Holy well of Our Lady, Ladywell St. May Day 'Obby 'Oss Festival. Museum. Shipwreck Museum. Prideaux Place house (open to the public).Rick Stein Fish Restaurant, Cookery School etc. Tourist office: Red Brick Building, North Quay. 01841-533449

| Pantersbridge | PANT'us'bridge | 5.5m E Bodmin off A38 | Bridge of Jesus |

Detail: 15C two-arched bridge

| Par | PAH | 3m E St. Austell on A3082 | From porth - harbour, little cove or landing. |

Details: Church of St. Mary by G.E. Street 1848, has steeple, sedilia, stained glass by Wailes. Cornish cross shaft in churchyard with Roman lettering. Almshouses built by Jonathon Rashleigh in 1650 won conservation award in 1980.

Parc-an-Ithon	Park-an-EYE'thon	1.5m NW Helston off A394	Furze field
Parc Erissey	Park Ur'IS'ee	1.5m N Redruth off A30	Dry field
Park Bottom	Park BOTT'om	2m NW Redruth off A30	Bottom field
Park Head	Park Head	5.5m SW Padstow off B3276	From Park, a nearby farm
Paul	Paul	2m S Penzance off B3315	Church of St. Paul

Details: Paul, son of a Welsh chieftan, founded monasteries including St.Pol-de-Leon. He helped his sister, Sitofolla, find an area for prayer in Newlyn. Spaniards burnt church 1595. Famous for obelisk, set up in 1778 by Prince Lucien Bonaparte, to Dolly Pentreath, said to be the last person to converse in Cornish. Church, 15C, restored 1893,has piscina, monuments 1709 (in Cornish), 1784, 1810. Hutchens almshouses of 1709 near church. Three Cornish crosses in locality.

| Pawton Quoit | Poll'tun Koit | 2m SW Wadebridge off A39 | Pool farm |

Detail: Neolithic monument called Giant's Quoit

Paynter's Lane End	Painters LANE End	2m NW Redruth off A30	After Paynter family?
Paynter's Cross	Painter's Cross	3.5m N Saltash on A388	After Paynter family?
Pedn Men An Mere	Pedun'men'an'mear	.5m S Porthcurno off B3315	Great stone headland

Detail: Formerly called Talmena Point (Brow of a great hillside)

| Pedn-men-du | Pen'men'do | .5m W Sennen Cove off A30 | Black stone headland |
| Pelynt | P'lint | 3m NW Looe on B3359 | Parish of St. Nunet. Parish (plu) plus saint's name |

Details: St. Nonn was grand-daughter of King Broccan and mother of St. David. Church, 15C, 17C, restored 1882, has Tuscan columned granite arcade of 1680, nave ceiled wagon roof with bosses, Buller tomb chest 1616, slate memorials of 1589, 1630, 1634, 1654, 1675, Bishop Trelawny's chair & staff. Best known as the burial place in 1721 of Sir Jonathan Trelawny, celebrated Bishop of Exeter and Winchester. His house, Trelawne, is near village. St. Nonna's well 1.25m NE. Barrow cemetery .5m SW.

Penair	P'NAIR	.5m NE Truro off A39	Hill top
Penare	P'NAIR	3m S Mevagissey from B3273	Headland (now Dodman Point)
Penarrow Point	Pn'ARROW Point	.5m E Mylor Churchtown off A39	Acre headland

| Penbeagle | Pn'BEE'gl | South Eastern fringe of St. Ives off B3306 | Top of small hill |
| Penberth | Pn'BERTH | 2.5m SW St. Buryan off B3315 | Bush end |

Details: Garden open occasionally

| Penberth Cove | Pn'BERTH cove | 2m SW St. Buryan off B3283 | Bush end cove |
| Pencalenick | Pen'kl'EN'ick | 2m E Truro off A39 near River Tresillian | End of the holly grove |

Details: House owned by 18C playwright Samuel Foote, rebuilt 1881 by J.P.St. Aubyn, now school.

| Pencarrow | Pen'CARROW | 3m NW Bodmin off A389 | Head of a valley with a fortified round (or deer park) |

Details: Georgian house & gardens, play area. Molesworth St. Aubyn family. Open to public.

| Pencarrow Head | Pen'CARRO Head | 2m SE Fowey via Bodinnick Ferry | Stag's head (from resemblance to horns) |
| Pencoys | Pen'COYZ (to rhyme with boys) | 3m SW Redruth on B3297 | End of a wood |

Details: Church, 1881, lancet style.

| Pencrebar | Pen'CREE'bar | 1m SW Callington on A390 | Facing the crest? |

Details: House originally called Crebar, but 'Pen' added by Foot family

| Pendarves | Pen'DAR'viss | 1.5m SW Camborne on B3303 | End of an oak wood |
| Pendeen | Pen'DEEN | 2.25m NE St. Just on B3306 | Cliff castle headland |

Details: Name now refers to the mining village, but was originally the headland, now called Pendeen Watch. Geevor Tin Mine, Lighthouse, Trevithick Trust. Church of St. John 1851, designed by Rev. Robert Aitken built by miners under his direction. Fogou in yard of Pendeen Manor Farm.

| Pendennis Point | Pen'DEN'iss Point | in SE Falmouth off A39 | Cliff castle headland. |

Details: Castle, 1544 built by Henry VIII, open to public. English Heritage.

Penderleath	Pen'der'LEETH	2m SW St. Ives off B3311	Top of farm by an old slab stone
Pendoggett	Pen'DOG'it	5m NE Wadebridge on B3314	Top of two woods
Pendrift	Pen'DRIFT or Pen'DREE	5m NE Bodmin off A30 Blisland	Top of the village near Jubilee Rock.
Penelewey	Pen'a'LOO'ee	2.5m S Truro on B3289	Top of Dewi's marsh or top of a place with elms
Penfound	Pen'found	4m SE Bude off A39	Beech end

Detail: Penfound Manor said to have the ghost of a young woman killed whilst trying to elope.

Pengegon	Pen'GEG'gun (hard g)	in SE fringe of Camborne off A3047	Ridge end?
Pengelly	Pen'GELLY	N fringe of Callington off A390 or A388	Grove end
Pengersick	Pen'GER'sick	5m W Helston off A394	End of marshy, reedy area

Detail: Pengersick Castle, 16c - open to public by appointment

Pengover Green	Pen'gover (as in 'of') Green	1.5m E Liskeard off A390	Stream head
Pengreep	Pen'GREEP	3m SE Redruth off A393	Ridge's end
Penhallam	Pn'HAL'um	5m S Bude, 1.5m W Week St.Mary off A39	End of moor. Manor ruins. English Heritage

Penhale	P'NAIL	6m SE Helston near Mullion on A3083	End of a moor
Penhale	P'NAIL	3.5m SW Newquay off A3075	End of moor
Penhale Point	P'NAIL Point	3.5m SW Newquay off A3075	Head of the marsh, from Penhale Farm

Details: Penhale Sands was earlier called Piran Sands from the patron saint of the parish

Penhale Jakes	P'NAIL Jakes	3m NW Helston off A394	End of a muddy moor
Penhallick	Pn'HAL'ick	1.5m E Camborne off A3047	End of the gorse moor

Detail: Mineral Tramways Discovery Centre at Old Cowlins Mill

Penhallow	Pn'HAL'o	5.5m NE St. Mawes off A3075	End of moor or marshy land
Penhallow	Pn'HAL'o	3.5m NE St. Agnes off A3075	End of moor or marshy land

Detail: Cider Farm.

Penhallow Moor	Pn'HAL'o Moor	5m SE Newquay off A30	End of moor or marshy land
Penhalurick	Pnal'UR'ick	3m S Redruth off B3297	End of marshy land with old rampart
Penhalvean	Pnl'VEEN	3.5m SE Redruth off B3297	Little head of the marsh (Little Penhale in 14C).
Penhalveor	Pnl'VEER	3.5m S Redruth off B3297	Great head of the marsh
Penjerrick	Pen'JERRICK	2m SW Falmouth off B3291	Head of a valley with a little strong stream

Detail: Semi- tropical gardens

Penlee Point	Pen'LEE Point	5m SE Torpoint off B3247	Headland with an old slab stone
Penmarth	Pen'MARTH	5m S Redruth off B3297	End of a high place or horse's head hill
Penmount	Pen'MOUNT	2m N Truro off A3076	Top of hill
Pennygillam	Penny'GILL'um (G as in Gill of fish)	1m SW Launceston off B3254	Head of a grove
Penpillick	Pen'PILL'ick	5m NE St. Austell on A390	Little Penpell

Detail: Penpell itself is a quarter of a mile away and means "far end".

Penpol	Pn'POLL	4m SW Truro off B3289	Head of the creek
Penpoll	Pen'POLL	2.5m NE Fowey off A390	Head of the creek
Penponds	Pen'PONS	1m SW Camborne off B3303	Bridge end

Detail: Church of Holy Trinity 1854, restored 1901 by J.P. St. Aubyn.

Penpont	Pen'PONT	7m SW Camelford off B3266	Bridge end
Penrice	Pen'RICE	S fringe of St. Austell off A390	Ford end

Detail: Penrice Longstone in Penrice School playing field, erected 2-3000BC, formerly Gwallon Downs

Penrose	Pn'ROSE	4.5m SW Padstow off B3274	End of the moorland
Penrose	Pn'ROSE	2m SW Helston off B3304	End of the moorland
Penryn	Pn'RIN (archaic Per'in)	1m NW Falmouth off A39	Promontory

Details: Court Leet in Saxon times; Domesday Survey of 1086, founded as borough 1216, Market charter in 1236 and Glasney Collegiate College 1265. Town Hall 1839, with museum. Georgian, and earlier, houses. Trelawney Public Garden. Harbour. Church at St. Gluvias to N (see separate entry). Centre of granite industry in 19C

Egyptian House
Chapel Street, Penzance

Pensilva	Pn'SIL'va	5m NE Liskeard off B3254	19C mining village with the invented name of Pen (plus silva), the name of local moorland Silva Down.
Penstowe	Pn'STO	5m NE Bude off A39	Chief place or end of Stowe estate
Penstraze	Pn'STRAZE	5m NW Truro off A390	End of a flat-bottomed valley
Pentewan	Pn'TOO'un (not Penty'won!)	4m S St. Austell off B32273	End of the River Tewyn or end of sand dunes or shore

Detail: Floating dock 1826. Railway 1829 - 1918.

| Pentillie Castle | Pn'TILL'y Castle | 3.5m N Saltash off A388 by River Tamar | Not known, but place called Tinnel to SE |

Details: 17C wing remains of house, landscaped by Repton, added to 19C, demolished 1968. Estate buildings at Paynters Cross include Regency villa.

Pentire	Pn'TEER (East and West)	2m W Newquay off B3282	Headland
Pentireglaze	P'n'teer GLAZE	3.5m NE Padstow off B3314	Green headland
Penventon	Pn'VEN'ton	W Redruth off A3047	Springhead
Penwartha	Pn'WARTH'a	1.5m S Perranporth off A3075	Higher end
Penweathers	Pn'WETHERS	1m SW Truro off A39	Trees End

| Penwerris | Pen'WERRIS | in N Falmouth off A39 | Hill end |

Detail: Church of St.Michael, 1827.

Penwith	PenWITH	Peninsula from Hayle to Lands End	End district
Penwithick	PenWITH'ick	2.5m N St.Austell off B3374	Top of a wooded place
Penzance	Pen'ZANCE or Pen'ZARNS	on A30	Holy headland (from ancient chapel of St. Mary).

Details: Sacked by Spanish 1595. Borough 1614, Coinage hall town 1663. Market House 1837, Georgian & Regency Chapel St, Union Hotel with remains of Georgian theatre, Wesleyan Chapel 1864, St. Mary's Church 1834 restored 1985, on site of ancient chapel with altar 1934 by Ernest Proctor. Cornish cross in churchyard. St. Paul's 1843, Baptist Chapel 1836. Penlee Art Gallery, Museum & park, Morrab Gardens (Cornish Cross), Morrab Library, Geological Museum, Maritime Museum, Lighthouse Centre, Jubilee Swimming Pool. Birthplace of Humphry Davy. Tourist Office: Station Road. 01736 - 362207

| Percuil | Per'KUAL | 1m NE St. Mawes off A3078 | Arrow cove |
| Perran-ar-worthal | Prn'ar'WERTH'l | 5m SW Truro off A39 | St. Piran in the manor of Arwothal beside a plain which floods. |

Details: St. Piran Church, Norman, 15C, rebuilt 1842, restored 1884, Norman tympanum. Holy well of St. Piran to E of Norway Inn.

| Perran Bay | Pr'an Bay | 6m SW Newquay off A3075 | Named after St. Piran |

Detail: Originally called Ligger Bay (from 'lig' seaweed).

| Perrancoombe | P'ran'COOM | 1m S Perranporth off A3075 | St. Piran's valley |
| Perranporth | P'ran'PORTH | 7m SW Newquay off A3075 | Piran's bay. |

Details: Harbour, cove and port of St. Piran's parish. St. Michael's church. Surfing, sand yachting, golf, boating lake. Perranzabuloe Folk Museum. Celtic Festival. Winston Graham wrote "Poldark" at Nampara Lodge. Information: 01872 - 573368.

| Perran Sands | P'ran Sands | 5.5m SE Penzance off A394 | From St. Piran |
| Perran Wharf | P'ran Warf | 5m SW Truro off A39 | From parish saint, St. Piran |

Details: Iron foundry rebuilt 1830 by Fox family. Iron arch dated 1791

| Perranuthnoe | Perra'NOOTH'no | 5m SE Penzance off A394 | Church of St. Piran in the Manor of Uthno. |

Details: Church, dedicated to St. Piran & St. Michael (other altars to the Virgin Mary and St. Nicholas), 15C & earlier, rebuilt 1883, has Norman doorways, 13C font in granite (one of few in Cornwall), roodloft stairs, squint, figure of St. James over S entrance from Goldsithney chapel. Sir Michael Tregorra, Rector 1427 - 33, was chaplain to Henry VI & Archbishop of Dublin.

Perranwell	Pr'an'WELL	2m SE Perranporth off A3075	St. Piran's well NE of Norway Inn
Perranwell Station	Pr'an'WELL Station	5m SW Truro off A39	St. Piran's well. Train stop on Falmouth - Truro line.
Perranzabuloe	Pr'n'ZAB'ulo	2m SE Perranporth off A3075	St. Piran in the sands - from sabulose (sandy).

Details: Oratory, erected 6c over saint's remains, buried by sand 9c, discovered 1835, concrete shelter built 1910. Second and third churches built and moved. Present church at Lambourne, built 1804, has 15C font, bench ends in screen, slate memorial 1675. Tall Cornish Cross in sands near ruins. Folk Museum. Holy well of St. Piran at Perranwell and another at Chiverton.

| Peterville | PETER'vill | in E St. Agnes off B3285 | Peter's ton (originally "grassland")? |

Phillack   **FILL'ack**   1m NE Hayle off A30   After St. Felek,
(name originally spelt with F)   Felicitas or Piala.

Details: The latter is said to be one of the Irish missionaries who landed in the Hayle estuary. Churchtown also called Egloshayle (church on an estuary). Church, 15C, rebuilt 1856, has part Norman capital in wall, sedilia, piscina, pulpit from rood screen, altar slab in table, linenfold panelling in sanctuary. Chi-Rho cross 5C in porch, inscribed stone. Cornish crosses in churchyard, rectory garden, nearby field etc. Coped stone near church. Holy well of St. Phillack S of church.

Philleigh   **FIL'ee**   5m SE Truro of A3078   After St. Fili or
moorland church

Details: St. Fili, honoured in Wales, was said to be a companion of St. Kea on the other bank of Fal. Church, 13C, 15C, rebuilt 1867, has 13C font, piscina, memorial 1680. Holy well to W at Tolverne.

Pill   **Pill**   5m SE Truro off B3289   Creek
Pillaton   **PILL'a'tun**   6m NW Saltash off A388   Post stakes farm

Details: Church, dedicated to St. Odulph, 15C, restored 1878, has old wagon roofs, large squint, two piscinas, aumbry, Royal Arms 1663, stocks, monument 1772. Clapper Bridge 1.25m NW late 15C.

Pine Lodge Gardens   **Pine Lodge Gardens**   at Cuddra 1m NE St. Austell off A390   From local pine trees? Woodlands, water features, marsh garden etc

Piper's Pool   **Pipers Pool**   5m W Launceston on A395   Named after local person?

Pigeon Ogo   **Pigeon O'go**   2m NW Lizard Point   Pigeon cave
Pits Mingle   **Pits Mingle**   .50m W Roche off B3274   Pit quarry
Place Manor   **Place Manor**   in NW Fowey off B3269   Large house

Detail: Ancestral home of Treffry family

Place Manor   **Place Manor**   1m SE St. Mawes (by ferry) off A3078   Large house

Detail: Spry Dalton family

Plain-An-Gwarry   **Plain'an' GWAR'ee**   in W Redruth off A3047   Playing place (see next entry)

Playing Place   **PLAY'ing Place**   2m SW Truro off A39   After medieval plain-an- gwarry (playing place or play arena) some traces of area survive. Holy well once located near almshouses.

Polapit Tamar   **POL'a'pit Tamer**   4m N Launceston off B3254   Pool pit, or corruption of bull's pit (nearby Bullapit).

Detail: Museum of wind and water mills

Polbathic   **Pol'BATH'ick** (as in Kath)   5m SW Saltash off A387   Boar's pool, or after a stream named Barthek?
Poldhu Point   **Pol'DUE Point**   6m S Helston off A3083   Black pool

Detail: Marconi memorial on cliff.

Poldowrian   **Pol'DOWER'ee'an**   2.5m SW Coverack off B3293   Watery place end

Detail: Museum of Pre-History. Garden.

Poleys Bridge   **PO'lees Bridge?**   1.5m NW Blisland off A30   After family of that name?

Detail: Five arches of large granite slabs built 1848

Polgear   **Pol'GEAR**   4m SE Redruth off B3297   Pool by a camp
Polgooth   **Pol'GOOTH**   2m SW St. Austell off A390   Goose pool or watercourse pool
Polkerris   **Pol'KE'riss**   5m E St. Austell off A3082   Heron's cove or fortified cove
Polmanter Water   **Pol'MANT'er Water**   1.5m SW St. Ives off B3311   Gateway to water?

| Polmarth | Pol'MARTH | 4.5m S Redruth on B3297 | Horse pool or Mark's pool |
| Polmassick | Pol'MASS'ick | 6m SW St. Austell off B3287 | Bridge of Madoc. |

Detail: Vineyard.

| Polmorla | Pol'MOR'la | 1.5m SW Wadebridge off A39 | Pool in place by the sea or sea marsh |
| Polperro | Pol'PERRO | 4m SW Looe off A387 | Pera's or Peter's harbour |

Details: Picturesque village. Church of St. John the Baptist 1838, chapel of ease to Lansallos. Jonathan Couch's House Museum. Holy well of St. Peter at Landaviddy. Art gallery.

| Polridmouth | PRID'muth | 5m SE St. Austell off A3082 | Cove with stone ford? |
| Polruan | Pol'ROO'un | 1m SE Fowey (across river) | Ruan's harbour (or seal cove?) |

Detail: 15C/16C artillery blockhouse. Holy well of St. Saviour by remains of chapel. Cornish Cross top of Fore St.

| Poltesco | Pol'TES'co | 1m NE Cadgwith off A3083 | Mossy pool. |

Details: Millhouse 1785. Ruins of serpentine factory.

| Polurrian Cove | Pol'LURE'ian Cove | .5m W Mullion off B3296 | Cress beds |
| Polwhele | Pol'WEEL | 2m NE Truro off A3076 | Pool in field or pool of beetles |

Details: House of the Polwhele family, including the Rev. Richard Polwhele, historian & author (1759 - 1838) has later 19C additions, now private school.

| Polwheveral | Pol'WER-vel? | .5m SE Constantine | Upper lively pool |
| Polyphant | Pol'IF'ent | 5.5m SW Launceston off A30 | Toad's or spring pool |

Detail: Quarry produces dark green easily worked stone.

| Polzeath | Pol'ZETH | 6.5m NW Wadebridge off B3314 | Dry pool |

Details: Iron age cliff castle (National Trust). John Betjeman buried at St. Enodoc. Information: 01208 - 862488.

Ponsandane	Pons'an'DANE	in E Penzance near Chyandour off A30	Man's bridge
Ponson Joppa	Pons'an SHOP'a?	1.5m SE Mullion on A3083	Workshop by bridge
Ponsanooth	Pons'a'NOOTH	3m NW Penryn off A393	Goose or stream bridge

Detail:19C Methodist Chapel

Ponsongath	Pons'an'GATH	2m SW Coverack off B3293	Cat's bridge
Ponts Mill	PONTS'mill	4.5m NE St. Austell off A390	Mill Bridge
Pool	Pool	2m W Redruth off A3047	Pool.

Details: Birthplace of Richard Trevithick. Cornish mines and beam engines,National Trust & Trevithick Trust. Trevenson Chapel 1809, delicate cast iron window tracery. Industrial Discovery Centre. Cornwall College and Camborne School of Mines, Geological Museum.

| Port Eliot | Port Ell'y'it | 3.5m E Saltash on B3249 | House of the Earls of St. Germans (Eliot family) |

Details: Originally Priory of St. Germans 13C undercroft & refectory still exists. Some 18C parts, but house mainly Sir John Soane 1806, W wing and porch H. Harrison 1829. Grounds laid out by Repton. Not open to public.

| Porkellis | P'KELLIS | 5m NE Helston off B3297 | Hidden pass or haven |
| Port Gaverne | Port'GAV'un (or Gayvun, as in 'raven') | 7m N Wadebridge off B3267 | Cove of a young goat or Gavran's cove. |

Details: Seigning and trading port, fish cellars

| Porth | Porth | in N Newquay off B3276 | Cove or harbour |
| Porthallow | Porth'AL'lo or Pra'LA | 9m SE Helston off B3293 | Alaw's cove or water lily stream |

| Porthcothan Bay | Porth'COTH'en Bay | 5m SW Padstow off B3276 | Cove named after nearby hamlet |
| Porthcurno | Porth'KERN'o | 3m SW St. Buryan off B3315 | Curno's cove or Cove of Horns, from cliff formation |

Details: Museum of Submarine Telegraphy, Trevithick Trust. Minack Theatre and Centre. Remains of early oratory in sands.

| Porthenalls | Porth'n'ALLS | 3m SE Marazion off A394 | Cliff cove near Prussia Cove. |

Details: House 1914 by Philip Tilden. Prussia Cove International Musicians Seminar.

| Porthgwarra | Port'GWARRA | 2.5m SE Land's End off B3315 | Higher cove (earlier hazel tree cove) |

Detail: Once known as Sweetheart's Cove from tale of thwarted lovers

| Porthgwidden | Porth'GWID'n | 4.5m S Truro off B3289 | White cove |

Detail: House built 1830 for Edmund Turner MP for Truro 1837-47. Now private flats.

| Porthgwidden | Porth'GWID'n | N fringe St. Ives off B3306 | White cove |
| Porth Joke | Porth JAWK (sometimes Polly Joke) | 2.5m SW Newquay off A3075 | |

Details: Chough's cove or bay with creek and plants (see Holywell Bay)

| Porthilly | Port'HILL'ee | 1.5m E Padstow off B3314 | Saltwater cove |

Details: Church of St. Michael. Norman, 13C 15C, restored 1867, has lancet window, rood screen, pulpit with linenfold panelling. Unusual Cornish cross.

| Port Isaac | Port'EYE'sik (originally Port IZZ'eck) | 6m NE Padstow on B3267 off B3314 | Corn or chaff port or unknown personal name (some suggest Jacob's Well)? |

Details: Once had second largest pilchard fishery on north coast and good slate trade. St. Peter's Church 1889. Holy well of St. Illick 2m NE.

| Porth Kidney | Port ID'nee | 1.5m NW Hayle off A3074 | Farewell cove |

Porthkea	Porth'KEY	1.5m S Truro off A39	On the way to Kea (porth as gateway or entrance).
Porthledden	Porth LED'n	1m NW St. Just off B3306	Wide cove
Porthleven	Port'LEVEN	2m SW Helston on B3304	Harbour on the Leven stream

Details: Older residents talk of "going down Port". St. Bartholomew Church 1841, remodelled 1893, Lady Chapel 1934 C.R. Corfield, vestry 1962.Harbour opened 1825, Old Customs House, West Wharf warehouse early 19C, shipyard,old lifeboat house, fishing. Giant's Rock W.

Porthmeor	Porth'MEAR	5.5m SW St. Ives on B3306	Great cove
Porthminster	Porth MIN'ster (beach)	SE fringe of St. Ives on A3074	Cove by an endowed church
Porth Navas	Port NAV'as	4.5m SW Falmouth off A394 (by Helford River)	Sheep's cove
Portholland	Port'HOLL'and	8.5m SW St. Austell off A3078	Cove of River Alan or old holy place.
Porthoustock	Porth'OW'stock or PROW'stek	7m S Falmouth off B3293	Ustick's cove
Porthpean	Porth'PEEN	1.5m S St. Austell off A390	Little harbour Chapel of St. Levan, 1884.
Porthtowan	Porth'TOW'n	4m N Redruth off A30	Cove of sand dunes or Towan cove
Portloe	Port'LO	8m SE Truro off A3078	Cove inlet
Portmellon	Port'MELL'un	6m S St. Austell off B3273	Mill or yellow cove
Portquin	Port'Gwin	5m N Wadebridge off B3314	White cove

Details: Fishing and trading port, fish cellars. Doyden Castle to W is 19C folly. National Trust.

Portreath	Por'TREETH (not Port'wreath!)	3m NW Redruth on B3300	Treath cove or sandy cove

Details: Mineral port and tramway with incline (pier begun 1760). St. Mary's Church 1841 by Wightwick.

Portscatho	Port'SCATH'o, Per'SCATH'a or Scatha	7m SE Truro off A3078	Harbour of boats
Portwrinkle	Port'RINK'l	6m SW Torpoint on B3247	Cove by Trewikkel farm
Poughill	PUFF'il or POF'l	1.5m NE Bude off A39	Poha's spring.

Details: Church, dedicated to St. Olaf (King Olaf of Norway), born 95AD, killed in battle with rebellious pagans 1030,14C 15C, restored 1889, has 14C N aisle, 14C tracery in E window, wagon roofs, old bench ends & seats, Royal Arms, wall paintings, tablet to Goldsworthy Gurney. Register book 1537 said to be oldest in Cornwall.

Poundstock	POUND'stock	4m S Bude off A39	Cattle pound settlement

Details: Church dedicated to Winnwaloe(says church guide book),though other sources say St. Neot. The saint, thought to be Cornish, founded a monastery at Landevennec. Very austere, he dressed in goats' hair clothes & slept on hard boards with a stone for a pillow. Church 14C, 15C, restored 1896, has some Norman masonry, 13C font, bench ends, interesting wall paintings, Jacobean pulpit. Ghost of 14C murdered priest. Unique 14C Guildhouse still in use. Holy well of St. Neot SW of church.

Praa Sands	Pray Sands	5m W Helston off A394	Witch's or hag's cove.
Praze-an-Beeble	Praise'an'BEE'bl	3m SW Camborne on B3303	The pipe field

Predannack Wollas	**Pr'DAN'ick Wollis** or **PRAD'neck**	7m SW Helston off B3296	Headland of Britain (name might have been given to the whole of the Lizard peninsula originally)
Presingoll	**Press'in'goll**	.75m S St. Agnes on B3277	Hazel tree copse

Detail: Shopping centre

Prideaux	**PRIDicks**	3m NE St. Austell off A390	Near the waters (Fr.pres d'eaux)

Detail: Iron Age fort nearby

Prideaux Place	**Prid'o Place**	NW fringe of Padstow off B3276	After Prideaux family (from French 'pres d'eau' near water), formerly top of the farm.

Detail: Elizabethan & later house of great character. Open to the public.

Probus	**PRO'bus**	5m NE Truro off A390	Church of St. Probus

Details: He was an early British Christian, probably from Dorset. Church, dedicated to Sts. Probus & Grace, has chancel screen with Tudor translation of Latin 'Gracia et Probus', meaning Grace and Goodness, which may account for the dedication (in 1851 two skulls, male and female, found in reliquary near altar). 15C church built on Celtic monastic site, office of canons surviving until 1549. Handsome church restored 1851 & later, has richly decorated three-stage tower, tallest in Cornwall, painted chancel roof, bench ends in screen, piscina, sedilia, altar slab, mosaic reredos, brass 1514, memorial 1766, James II Royal Arms, stocks. Holy well of Sts Probus and Grace S of church. Holy Well of Fenton Barren 2m nw. Holy Well of Venton Glidder 1.5m N. Holy Well of Trelowthas 1m SW. Vicarage 1839 by Wightwick, Grammar School 1860 by Street. Duchy of Cornwall Garden, open to public. Trewithen House nearby (open to public).

Prospidnick	**Pros'PID'nick**	2m NW Helston off B3303	Pine tree thicket
Prussia Cove	**Prussia Cove**	6m W Helston off A394	From 18C smuggler

John Carter who worked from King's Cove so successfully he was nicknamed King of Prussia after Frederick the Great, much admired at the time.

Detail: Porthenalls House 1914. Prussia Cove International Musicians Seminar.

Pulla Cross	**PULLA Cross**	4m NW Penryn off A393	Pools near crossroads

Q

Quethiock	**KWITH'ick**	4m E Liskeard off A390	Wooded place

Details: Church, dedicated originally to Welsh St. Cadoc, then. St. Hugh of Lincoln, 14C 15C, restored 1879, has wagon roofs, painted ceiling, squint, reredos, brasses 1471 & 1631, stocks.Cross one of tallest in Cornwall.

Quies	**Gwis ?** (to rhyme with miss)	NW Padstow off B3276	Sow's rock
Quintrell Downs	**KWINTrell Downs**	2m SE Newquay on A392	From Quinterell family

Detail: Newquay Pearl Centre

R

Raginnis	**R'GIN'is**	3m S Penzance off B3315 (to rhyme with Guinness)	Facing the island (St. Clement's Isle off Mousehole)
Rame Head	**Rame Head**	4.5m S Torpoint off B3247	Headland, origin unknown - but maybe ram's head (English).

Details: St. Michael's Chapel, thought to be Norman and later.

Rame	RAME	3.75m S Torpoint off B3247	Reason for name not known

Details: Church, dedicated to St. Germanus, Bishop of Auxerre, Norman, 13C 14C 15C, restored 1885, has broach spire, Norman typanum, altar slab, piscinas, squint, wagon roof, bench ends, monuments 1677, 1733, 1799, headstones to sailors, coastguards, pilots etc. Polhawn Battery.

Rame	RAYM	3.5m W Penryn on A394	After Rame family?
Ramsgate	Ramsgit	1.5m SW Camborne on B3303	Not known
Ready Money Cove	Ready Money Cove	SW fringe of Fowey off A3082	Stone ford cove

Detail: Near. St. Catherine's Castle

Reawla	Roo'AR'la	4m SW Camborne off B3280	Royal place (from Norman French)
Redannick	R'DAN'ick	S fringe of Truro off A390	Fern brake
Redmoor	RED'more	2m NW Lostwithiel off B3269	Red marsh

Detail: Nature Reserve

Red River	Red River	River near Redruth	Named from the tin mining waste which coloured the water.

Details: In 16C it was called Dour Conor(River Conor), from the lost manor of Connerton. It runs from Brea village & winds NW to coast at Gwithian.

Redruth	R'DROOTH or DROOTH (archaic Rd'REETH)	on A30	Red ford from mining waste in Red River.

Details: Hill town, hey day in mining era. Late Georgian & Victorian buildings. Clock tower 1828, increased in height 1900. Wesleyan Chapel 1826, Quakers Meeting House 1833, St. Andrews Church 1883. St. Uny parish church SE of town rebuilt 1756. New Market Way with Tregellas Tapestry, Victorian style shops, converted from old market. New Cornish Centre. West End restoration and town garden. William Murdoch made first self-propelled high-pressure engine in 1784; gas-lit his house in Cross Street 1793 and lit Redruth's streets by gas (first in the world). Fanny Moody, Cornish Nightingale, born Redruth 1866. Home of Cornish Rugby (Bert Solomon played for England 1910). Cornish Goldsmiths.

Redruth Church Town	R'DROOTH Church Town	SW edge of Redruth.	Contains parish church of St. Uny (see separate entry under St. Uny), vicarage and cottages.
Reen Cross	Reen Cross	1.5m E Perranporth off A3075	Hillside
Rejerrah	R'JEH'ra	3.5m SW Newquay off A3075	Gorvoy's ford
Releath	R'LEETH	3.5m N Helston off B3297	Slab ford
Relubbas	R'LUB'us	6m NE Penzance on B3280	Lehoube's ford?
Rescorla	Res'COR'la	3.5m SW St.Austell off A390	Ford by sheepfold
Reskadinnick	Res'ka'DIN'ick	1m NW Camborne off A30	Ford by fortified place?
Reskymer	Res'SKIM'er	3m SE Helston off B3293	Ford where streams join
Resparva	R'SPAR'va	5.5m SE Newquay on A30	Inner or middle ford
Respryn Bridge	R'SPRINN Bridge	3m SE Bodmin off A38	Timber or crows' ford

Detail: Partly 15C

Name	Pronunciation	Location	Meaning
Restormel Castle	R'STOR'ml Castle	1m N Lostwithiel off A390	Rough land on bare rounded hill.

Details: Castle dates from 12c. English Heritage. The most perfect example of military architecture in Cornwall (Pevsner).

Name	Pronunciation	Location	Meaning
Restronguet	R'STRONG'git	2.5m NE Penryn off A39	Ford on a promontory wood
Resugga	Res'UGG'a	5m W St. Austell off A3058	Hillspur by a cave
Retallack	R'TAL'ick	5.5m SW Falmouth	The end of the marsh or Talek's heath
Retallack	R'TAL'ick (or Retallick)	2m NE St. Columb Major off B3274	Talek's heath or willows' ford.

Detail: Fishing lakes.

Name	Pronunciation	Location	Meaning
Retanna	R'TAN'a	5m W Penryn off A394	Narrow ford
Retew	R'TOO	5m SE St. Columb Major off A30	Black ford
Rezare	R'ZAIR	4.5m SE Launceston off A388	Ford by a fort

Detail: Holy well on village green

Name	Pronunciation	Location	Meaning
Rialton	Re'AL'tun	1.5m E Newquay on A3059	Royal place

Details: Wing of house has remains of 15C monastic manor, with chamber of Prior Vivian of Bodmin, who used it as his summer palace. Holy well and inscribed stone.

Name	Pronunciation	Location	Meaning
Rilla Mill	RILLa Mill	6m NE Liskeard off B3254	Mill belonging to Rillaton
Rillaton	RILL'a'ton	6.5m NE Liskeard off B3254 .5m N of Minions	Flat stone ford

Details: Early Bronze Age barrow where gold cup found 1837, now in British museum (copy in Royal Cornwall Museum)

Name	Pronunciation	Location	Meaning
Rinsey	RIN'zi	4m W Helston off A394	House on promontory
Rising Sun	Rising Sun	2.5m NE Callington off A390	Suggested so called because the area is on the southern slopes of Hingston Down and gets the morning sun coming up over Dartmoor.
Roche	Roach	5m NW St. Austell on B3274	From French for rock.

Details: Chapel of St. Michael (1409) on rock. Parish church dedicated to St. Gonand, 15C, rebuilt 1822, 1890, has Norman font. Cornish cross in churchyard (unusual wheel head) & rectory garden. Holy well of St. Gundred near Victoria Inn.

Name	Pronunciation	Location	Meaning
Rock	Rock	4.5m W Wadebridge off B3314 (Camel Estuary).	Originally Black Rock, but word 'black' has been lost
Rocky Valley	Rocky Valley	2m SW Boscastle off B3263	Rock

Detail: Carvings from Early Bronze Age

Name	Pronunciation	Location	Meaning
Roscarrack	Rus'CA'rick (Ca as in cat)	SW fringe of Falmouth	Cadoc's heath
Roscroggan	Rus'KROG'en	1m N Camborne off A30	Skull or shell heath
Rose	Rose	1.5m NE Perranporth off B3285	Roughland
Rose-an-Grouse	Rose-an-GROWZ	1.5m SW Hayle on A30	Heath of the cross
Rosecliston	Rus'CLISS'tun?	1.5m SW Newquay off A3075	Pebble ford

Detail: Holiday camping park

Rosecraddock	Rus'CRAD'uck	2m NE Liskeard on B3254	Caradoc's or Cradoc's heath or ford

Detail: Holiday village

Rose-in-Vale	Rose'in'Vale (Cornish Rawse)	1m E St. Agnes off B3285	Apple tree heath
Rose-in-The-Vale	Rose-in-The-Vale (Cornish Rawse)	3m SE Newquay off A3058	Apple tree heath
Roseland Peninsula	Roseland Peninsular	between Truro and St. Mawes	Promontory

Detail: Roseland Visitor Centre at St. Mawes 01326-270440

Rosemanowes	Rus'men'awes	3m NW Penryn off A394	Hill of awl-shaped rocks

Detail: Hot Earth Project

Rosemerryn	Rus'ME'rin	2m SW Falmouth	Merin's hillspur
Rosemorran	Rus'MO'ren	1.5m NE Penzance off B3311	Blackberry heath

Detail: Farmhouse, with longest span of thatch in Cornwall, 18C on earlier foundations, has Cornish Cross and Holy Well.

Rosemullion Head	Rus'MULLION Head	3m S Falmouth nr Mawnan Smith	Milyan's or clover headland
Rosemundy	Ros'MUN'gi	S fringe of St. Agnes off B3277	Mineral (ore) house on roughland
Rosenannon	Rus'NAN'un	3m NE St. Columb Major off B3274	Heath with ash trees

Detail: Holy Well of the Chapel of St. Mary Magdalene .75m N

Rosevean	Rus'VEEN	3.5m N St. Austell off B3374	Little heath
Rosevear	Rus'veer	3.5m SE Helston on B3293	Great heath
Rosevidney	Ros'VID'nee?	2.5m SW Hayle	Coarse grass, moor or sedge moor
Rosewarne	Rose-WARN	N fringe of Camborne on A30	Heath with alder trees

Detail: Training centre

Roseworthy	Rez'WORTH'i, R'ZURRY or ZURRY	2.5m W Camborne off A30	Gorhi's ford

Detail: Holy well (remains) .5m S of Roseworthy Barton

Roskear	Rus'KEER	in NE Camborne off A30	Ford by a fort
Roskrow	Rus'KROW (rhyme with 'cow')	1.5m NW Penryn off A39	Hut on roughland

Details: Original manor dates to 11C, but 17C house (home of Mrs Delany, famous 18C flower artist, and also used for French prisoners of war) burnt down 1890.Duke of Windsor & Mrs. Simpson stayed in rebuilt house.

Rosudgeon	Rus'UDG'n	5m E Penzance on A394	Roughland for oxen
Rough Tor	ROW'ter (to rhyme with doubter)	3m SE Camelford (Bodmin Moor) off A39	Rough crag.

Details: Bronze Age round houses & cairns. Foundation of ancient chapel in base of war memorial, Holy well of St. Michael said to be a few hundred yards below. National Trust

Round Ring	Round Ring	N fringe of Penryn off A39	Plain-an-Gwary or Playing Place
Roundwood Quay	Roundwood Quay	3m SE Truro off A39	Built round a wood?

Details: Iron Age camp, shipping point for tin and copper in 18c with refining buildings & lime kiln, later shipbuilding and coalyard. National Trust.

Gatehouse at Trenethick Barton, Helston

Row	Ro	at St. Breward off A39	Row of 19C cottages
Ruan High Lanes	Roo'an HIGH Lanes	6m SE Truro on A3078	From St. Ruan
Ruan Lanihorne	Roo'an LANN'i'horn	4.5m SE Truro off A3078	St. Ruan at Rihoarn's church site.

Details: Relics of saint, possibly Glastonbury monk, moved to Tavistock Abbey. Church, Norman, 13C 14C 15C, restored 1866, has some Norman masonry,13C priest effigy, sedilia, squint, bench ends inorporated in pulpit.Holy well of St. Ruan W of church. Rectory William White 1850.

| Ruan Major | Ruan Major | 2.5m N Lizard off A3083 | From St. Ruan |

Details: Church,15C restored 1866, has tower chequered with granite & serpentine. Now deserted.

| Ruan Minor | Roo'an Minor | 2m NE Lizard Village off A3083 | from St. Ruan |

Details: Small church, 14C 15C, restored 1854, has 13C piscina, serpentine blocks in walls. Holy well

| Rumford | RUM'ford | 3.5m SW Wadebridge off B3274 | Wide ford |
| Rumps Point | Rumps Point | 7m NW Wadebridge off B3314 | (Near Polzeath) Twin-rump shape |

Details: Iron Age cliff castle

| Ruthenbridge | Ruth'n'bridge (ruth as in first part of mother) | 4m W Bodmin off A389 | Bridge over red river |

Detail: Early 15C bridge over the Ruthern stream

| Ruthvoes | Ruthers (to rhyme with brothers) | 2m SE St. Columb Major off A30 | Red dyke |

Details: St. Columb, an Irish pagan princess who saw the Holy Ghost in the form of a dove when she became a Christian. She fled to Cornwall to escape marriage to a pagan prince, but because she refused to marry him or renounce her faith, he beheaded her. It is said that where her blood fell a stream appeared, which was declared a Holy well. Miniature Pony Centre, Spring fields

S

| Saltash | Salt'ASH | Town on A38 | Ash(tree), with later addition of salt (local production). |

Details: 12C port, ancient borough(13C charter), gateway to Cornwall via Brunel's railbridge of 1859, Tamar roadbridge of 1962 (widened in 2001), with road tunnel on A38 built 1988. Parish church St. Stephens until 1881,then St. Nicholas and Faith (next to Town Hall of 1780) Norman and later, Mary Newman's Tudor cottage. Waterside development. Host to International and National Water-ski Championships. Annual regatta and Winkle Fair. Saltash Sailing Club, Caradon Gig Club (world champions).Once base of largest river steamer fleet in S. West. Youth Centre (Livewire Project). Elliott's (preserved old fashioned grocery shop). Information Centre 01752 266030

| Saltmill | Salt'mill | N fringe of Saltash off A38 on Salt mill creek | Salt mill for local salt production |
| Samson | Samsun | 2m NW St. Mary's | From St. Samson (see entry under Golant) Thought to be the remains of a chapel. |

Details: On North Hill are twelve megalithic tombs beneath round barrows. On South Hill are four similar graves.

| Sancreed | San'creed or San'cred | 3.5m W Penzance off A30 | After St. Sancred. |

Details: There were two saints of this name, one was a disciple of St. Petroc, and the other, an Irishman, was said to have accidentally killed his father, then, in contrition lived as a swineherd, becoming revered for curing pigs' diseases. Church,14C 15C, restored 1891, has 14C font, piscina, rood screen, wagon roof in porch, stoup. Holy well and baptistery WSW of church. Five Cornish crosses, two with unusual decorations and inscriptions. Burial place of Stanhope Forbes. Carn Euny Ancient Village, English Heritage.

Sandplace	SAND'place	2.5m N Looe on A387/B3254 (on East Looe River)	Place for bringing sea-sand as fertiliser for fields.
Saveock	Sev'ee'OCK	4m W Truro off A390	Strawberry place
Scilly Isles (see Isles of Scilly)			Probably from Roman goddess Sulis
Sconner	SCON'er	5m SW Saltash on A374	Conor's heath
Scorrier	SKO're'er (short 'o')	2m NE Redruth on A3047	Place with iron-quartz vein and mining waste (from Latin scoria).

Details: Scorrier House, 19C rebuild of earlier house. Two Cornish crosses, one with unusual figure, from Rame, nr Penryn.

| Seaton | SEE'tun | 4m E Looe off B3247 | At mouth of River Seaton (from seth, arrow-like, or seythen, twisting) |

Detail: Monkey Sanctuary along coast

Sennen and Sennen's Cove SEN'un — 8m SW Penzance on A30 — From patron saint, St. Senan, thought to be either an unknown female Cornish or Welsh saint, or an Irish abbot saint.

Details: The Lord of Ganilly, a survivor from the lost land of Lyonesse, is said to have landed in the cove and built a chapel following his deliverance. Church, 13C 15C, restored 1867, has 13C window in N transept, 13C Virgin & Child figure, remains of wall painting? Cornish crosses in churchyard, cemetery & at Sennen Green. Roundhouse.

Name	Pronunciation	Location	Meaning
Seworgan	**S'VOR'gn**	3.5m NE Helston off A394	Goethgen's ford
Sharptor	**Sharp'ter**	5.5m NE Liskeard off B3254	Sharp outcrop
Sheffield	**Sheffield**	2.5m S Penzance off A30 on B3315	Sheffield Terrace mentioned in Paul Tithe Apportionment
Sheviock	**Shev'uck**	4.5m W Torpoint on A374	Place of strawberries

Details: Church of St. Peter & St. Paul, 13C 14C, restored 1851, 1872, has 13C font, sedilia, piscina, 14C s. transept, 14C five-light E window with statue niches, twin funeral recesses and tomb chests with figures of 1370, wagon roof, bench ends, stocks. Cornish Cross .25m W. Holy Lady well to SE.

Name	Pronunciation	Location	Meaning
Shop	**Shop**	W St. Merryn on B3276	From Parken's workshop

Detail: Surname found in parish from early 16C.

Name	Pronunciation	Location	Meaning
Shop	**Shop**	2m E Morwenstow off A39	From workshop or smithy (found in 1840)
Shortlanesend	**Short'lanes'END**	2m NW Truro on B3284	After local family called Shorte?

Detail: Pen founder nearby means 'the end of the lane'.

Name	Pronunciation	Location	Meaning
Shortacross	**SHORT'a'cross**	3.5m NE Looe of A387	Short way from crossroads?
Siblyback Reservoir	**Sibb'lee'back Reservoir**	4m NW Liskeard off B3254	Land ridge of family called Sibly, later made into reservoir

Details: Sailing, fishing, walking, visitor centre.

Name	Pronunciation	Location	Meaning
Sinns Barton	**Sins BAR'tun**	2m N Redruth off Porthtowan Road	Not known

Details: Ruins of 15C chapel and All Saints Holy Well.

Name	Pronunciation	Location	Meaning
Sithney	**SITH'ni** (originally Sinny)	2m NW Helston off B3302	From patron saint of church St. Sitheny

Details: The saint also venerated in Brittany, where he was patron saint of mad dogs. Believed buried at Sithney in 1478. Church, Norman, 15C, has Norman jamb stones in porch & other masonry, coffin slab 1240, cusped 14C window in N aisle, piscina, pillar erected 1741 by Dr. Oliver, inventor of Bath Oliver biscuits, to his father. Their 16C house has large collection of coniferous trees.

Name	Pronunciation	Location	Meaning
Skewes	**Skoos?**	4m NE St. Columb Major off B3274	Elder bushes or shaded place
Skinners Bottom	**Skinners Bottom**	3m NE Redruth off A30	Probably from family named Skinner
Sladesbridge	**SLADES'bridge**	1.5m SE Wadebridge on A389 (River Allen)	Shallow valley or from family named Slade?
Slaughterbridge	**SLAUGHTER' bridge**	1.5m N Camelford on B33144 (River Camel)	From battles of 540 & 823.

Details: Stone, 9ft in length, with carved lettering, circa AD540, by River Camel. Arthurian Centre near bridge. Condolden Barrow located nearby.

Richard Trevithick's cottage at Higher Penponds, Camborne.

This thatched roof cottage was where one of Cornwall's most distinguished sons lived as a boy, and later spent much of his married life with Jane and their children. Voted the top of a poll of the greatest Cornish men and women in the Western Morning News in 2002, his inventions included the first road locomotive. Denied proper recognition in his lifetime, he died in poverty in Dartford in 1833.

South Hill	South'ill	3m NW Callington	Daughter church of North Hill (originally North Hindle meaning hinds' wood) or Old English south hyll (south hill) (See North Hill).

Details: Church, dedicated to St. Sampson, a Welsh noble abbot-bishop who founded monasteries in Ireland, Cornwall and Brittany (see entry for Golant), 14C, 15C, restored 1871, has tower with parapet supported by 12 apostles, ogee arched tomb recesses, sedilia, piscina, wagon roof, slate memorials 1507, 1663, inscribed stone with chi-rho monogram (early Christian symbol based on first two letters of Greek Christos - XP) in churchyard. Holy well of Manaton SE of church.

South Petherwin	South PETHER'win	2m SW Launceston on B3254	From patron saint St. Padern plus 'gwynn' meaning blessed.

Details: The saint may have been a Welsh abbot-bishop or local chieftain, father of St. Constantine. (See North Petherwin). Church, Norman, 15C restored 1889,has Norman N door, capital & stoup(said to be only one in Cornwall), 13C font, sepulchral slabs in tower, 15C altar slab, wagon roofs, tower screen, pulpit 1631, James 1 Royal Arms. .75m SW Holy well of Manaton.

South Pill	South PILL	N fringe of Saltash on B32371	South creek
South Wheatley	South WEET'lee	7m NW Launceston off B3254	Bright clearing
Sparnock	SPAR'nuck	2.5m SW Truro	Thorny place
Sparnon Gate	SPARnun Gate	1.5m NW Redruth off A30 or B3300	Thorny place
Splatt	Splat	4m NW Wadebridge off B3314 near Rock	Plot of land
Splattenridden	Splat'an'RID'n	2m SW Hayle off A30	Bracken plot
Stamps and Jowl Zawn	Stamps and Jowl Zawn	1.5m W Pendeen off B3306 on coast	Devil's stamping mill
Stannon	Stan'dun	3m NE St. Breward off B3266	Stone hill (from OE'stan dun')

Detail: Bronze Age circle of 76 stones

Stenalees	Sten'a'LEEZ	3m N St. Austell on A391	Grey- green tin work or tin-working ruins
Stennack	STEN'ack	S fringe of St. Ives	Tin stream work
Stepaside	STEP'a'side	5m NW St. Austell off A3058	Steep place? (from English stepel)
Stibb	Stibb	3.5m NE Bude off A39	Tree stump
Sticker	Sticker	3.5m SW St. Austell off A390	Tree stumps
Stithians	Stithy'uns (originally STIDy'uns)	3.5m NW Penryn off A393	From female parish saint St. Stediana, about whom little known.

Details: Church, mainly 14C & 15C, restored 1862 & 1873, has good granite ashlar tower, 14C N aisle, piscina on Norman corbel,16C brass admonition tablet, Georgian pulpit. Cornish crosses in churchyard and vicarage garden. Lady Holy well 1m NE at Kennal Vale. Annual Agricultural Show in July.

Stoke Climsland	Stoke CLIMS'land	3m N Callington off A388	Outlying farm in the manor of Climsom or 'chief place in Clement's land' (according to the Rev. Martin Andrews, Rector from 1921)

Details: Church, dedicated to St. Faith, a French virgin martyr burnt to death in AD303, is 13C, 15C, restored 1860,and has wagon roofs, 14C piscina, slate memorials 1605 1623, Lady Chapel curtains & frontal material from Coronation of Elizabeth 11. The church has had close links with royalty since the patronage of the Earl of Cornwall in 1265. 1.25m NW site of Holy well of St. Mallett. Horse Bridge 2.5m E 1437 with seven arches.

Stoketon	STOKE'tun	3m NW Saltash off A38	Outlying farm
Stoptide	STOP'tide	4m NW Wadebridge off B3314	Place where tide reached
Stowe	Stowe	1.75m NW Bude off A39	Place of assembly or holy place

Details: Remains of Stowe House, built 1680 by John Grenville, Earl of Bath, pulled down 1739, much material used in Stowe Barton, its successor.

Stratton	STRAT'un	.5m NE Bude on A39	Valley of the River Neet

Details: Fine church dedicated to St.Andrew, 14C 15C, restored 1888, has wagon roofs, bench ends, Jacobean pulpit, 14C effigy of knight,brass 1561 to Sir John Arundell of Trerice, Burne-Jones E window, rood screen 1901. Cornish Giant, Anthony Payne, born here.

Stripple Stones	Stripple Stones	3m SE St. Breward off A30	Not known

Details: Neolithic henge and stone circle. .75m W is Trippet Stones circle.

Stowe's Pound	Stowe's Pound	1m N Minions off B3254	After Stowe family?

Detail: Bronze Age fortification of piled stones

Summercourt	SUMMA'court	5m SE Newquay on A3058/A30	Summer courtyard?

Detail: Dairy Land Farm Museum

Swanpool	Swanpool	SW fringe of Falmouth	Swan sanctuary, said to have been the swannery of the Killigrew family
Sweetshouse	SWEETS'ouse	3.5m SE Bodmin on B3269	After family called Sweet?

SAINTS

Saints' Way   Footpath from Padstow to Fowey. 26 mile path

Details: The path follows the route of the Celtic saints going from Ireland and Wales to Brittany. It includes St. Breock, Helman Tor, Tywardreath and Golant.

St. Agnes   S'nt AGG'ness   5.5m NE Redruth on B3277   From St. Agnes

Details: She was a young 4C girl martyred in Rome by stabbing in the throat. Church, rebuilt 1846 by J.P. St. Aubyn; bases of Norman chapel & 1482 piers found 1931, stone of altar from old quay. Cornish cross. Holy well of St. Agnes at Chapel Porth (no stone remains). RC church 1882 by Cowill, Drewitt & Wheatly of Truro. 19C mining and shipbuilding centre. Museum. Craft workshops and galleries. Information: 20 Churchtown 01872 - 554150.

St. Agnes, Isles of Scilly	locally called AGG'nes	3m SW St. Mary's	Pasture headland or grazing enclosure.

Details: Church, built early 19C, has nave & western tower. Holy well of St. Warna 6C, said to be patron saint of shipwrecked sailors, sailed from Ireland in ittle boat. Former lighthouse 1680. Parish museum. Cairn cemetery, Priest's Rock and Troy Town Maze.

Old house at St. Columb Major

St. Allen   **S'nt AL'un**   3.5m N Truro off   Named after St. Alun
                                  A30 & A39

<u>Details:</u> The saint was thought to be either a Welsh saint, who became Bishop of Quimper, or a Breton saint. Church, 15C, has good 13C doorway, 13C tombstone, piscina, slate memorials 1626 1657. Former incumbent, Sir Harry Trelawny, changed faiths three times. Four Cornish crosses in area.

St. Ann's Chapel **S'nt ANN's**   3m NE Callington just   After St. Ann.
                      Chapel   off A390

<u>Details:</u> St. Ann was the mother of the Virgin Mary. There are two wells of St. Ann's, and an earlier well of St. Andrew, patron saint of the parish church at Calstock.

St. Antony in   **S'nt AN'tony in**   5m SW Falmouth off B3293 Patron saint was
Meneage   **Men'EEG**   at Gillan Creek.   Cornish king and
                                                          martyr St. Entinen
                                                          (Antonius in Latin).

<u>Details:</u> Church 12-15C, restored 1890, has 12C nave, chancel & S transept, 13C chancel lancet window, 13C stoup, 15C N aisle & West tower, brass chandeliers, dog door. Holy well of St. Anthony near church.

St. Anthony in   **S'nt AN'tony in**   1m SE St. Mawes by ferry Patron saint was
Roseland   **Roseland**   Cornish king and
                                                            martyr St. Entinen
                                                          (Antonius in Latin).

<u>Details:</u> Best example of a parish church in 12C or 13C (Pevsner), restored 1850, has Norman S doorway & nave, piscinas, memorials to Spry family, entrance to Place House (1840, neo-Gothic). Holy well of St Anthony nearby.

St. Austell	S'nt OR'stull	On A390	After St. Austol
	(archaic: Sint Os'tl)		

Details: Cornwall's largest conurbation. Church dedicated to St. Austolus,a godson of St. Mewan.They were great friends,eventually dying within a week of each other. Holy Trinity Church, 13 - 15C, restored 1872, has tower with figures in niches & 24-hr clock, Norman piscina, wagon roofs, rood screen, 13C chapel, bench end with fox preaching to geese. Market House & Town Hall 1844 (on site of building of 1791), Quaker Meeting House 1829, Mengue Stone. Queens Head Hotel 17C. Old Liberal Club (1890) and Red Bank (1987) by Silvanus Trevail. Centre of china clay industry. Joseph Hodge, inventor of fire engine, born here. Brewery Visitor Centre. Cornish Market World. Information 01726 - 76333.

St. Benet's	S'nt BEN'ets	3m SW Bodmin on	After St. Benedict
		A389 near Lanivet	

Details: Founded as lazar hospital 1411, became Courtenay house 16C, additions 1859, now restaurant. St. Benedict's Chapel (remains).

St. Blazey	Sint BLAY'zi	3m E St. Austell on A390	From dedication to
			St. Blaise.

Details: The saint was an Armenian martyr of about 4AD, who helped people with throat problems and was patron saint of wool combers.Also known as 'holy place on beach' until silting up of tidal estuary. Church, built 1440, restored 1839 1897, has statue niche on tower, 17C slate memorial & monument to Henry Scobell, treasurer to Queen Anne. Early 19C Market House on granite columns. Tregrehan House, late Georgian, nearby.

St. Blazey Gate	S'nt BLAY'zi Gate	2m E St. Austell on A390.	See previous entry
St. Breock	S'nt BREE'uck	1m W Wadebridge off A39	From patron
			St. Breock.

Details: The Welsh saint,who studied under St.Germanus,converted his parents and with 168 disciples went to Brittany via Cornwall,leaving his name at St. Breoc. Earlier name of Nancent means valley of saints. Church,13C 14C 15C, restored 1881, has 13C N transept arch, 14C doorways and windows, 13C coffin lid, 15C font,old porch roofs, alabaster reredos 1908, brasses 1520-30,slate memorials 16C and 17C, including large slate monument to Prideaux Brune family, 1598. Pillar stone 1m SW with Roman inscription. Early Bronze Age longstone on downs and Bronze Age Nine Maidens row of stones. Giants Quoit.

St. Breward	S'nt BREW'd	7m NE Wadebridge off	From patron saint,
	(originally called	B3266, fringe	St. Brewerd.
	Simonward)	Bodmin Moor	

Details: Believed to be son of King Kenen, and companion to St.Samson. Church, Norman, 15C, restored 1864, has Norman piers, window,old wagon roofs, bench ends,screen, Royal Arms 1700, sundial 1792. Thomas Rowlandson painted Dr. Syntax there. Holy well of St. James SW of church. Cornish cusped cross head in cemetery. Stone and hut circles in nearby area.

St. Buryan	S'nt BER'ee'an	5m SW Penzance	From female Irish
		on B3283	saint, St. Beriana.

Details: She had healing powers, and is said to have cured the son of King Gerent of paralysis. Large church with tall tower, founded by King Athelstan in 930, collegiate church in 13C, mainly 15C, restored 1814, 1874, has two Norman arches,13C coffin monument,medieval rood screen, misericords, bench ends in desk. Cornish cross in churchyard, and others in locality. Holy Well at Alsia. Nearby Merry Maidens, Early Bronze Age standing stones, Tregiffian chambered tomb (Cornwall Heritage Trust).

St. Catherine	S'nt Catherine	at Temple 6m NE Bodmin	After St. Catherine.
		just off A30	

Details: On site of house of Knights Templars, who were succeeded by Knights Hospitallers of St. John of Jerusalem (patron was Catherine of Alexandria). Tiny church on moor, commandery in 12C, ruin in 18C with ash tree in nave, rebuilt 1883 by Sylvanus Trevail. After Order's dissolution became Crown property as well as venue for illicit marriages.

St. Cleer **S'nt KLEE'r** 2.5m N Liskeard From English patron
off B3254 saint, St. Clarus

Details: He had a shrine in Normandy, but was murdered at the behest of a besotted chieftainess when he refused her advances. Church,15C, restored 1877, has Norman N doorway,N arcade 1400,13C font, piscinas, squint, Royal Arms 1708, 17c painted panels. Holy well in 15C building with Cornish Cross. Doniert Stone, The Hurlers stone circles, The Pipers standing stones and Trethevy Quoit in area.

St. Clement **S'nt CLEM'nt** 1.5m SE Truro off A390 From patron saint,
St. Clemens

Details: He was a Roman 1C Pope. Maritime sites dedicated to him after he was martyred by being bound to an anchor and thrown in the sea. Church, 13 - 15C, restored 1865, has 13C lancet windows, 15C font, head stone to servant (who asked for reduced wages because age made her less able to work), stocks, lychgate with slate hanging. Cornish cross with early inscribed letters. Holy well of St. Clement E of church.

St. Clether **S'nt KLETH'er** 8m W Launceston From patron saint,
off A395 St. Cleder

Details: Believed to be one of the 24 offspring of King Broccan of Brecon. Church, Norman (three pier capitals remain), rebuilt 1865 in Early English style, apart from 15C tower, has two 15C bells. Holy well and chapel .25m NW of church, is largest in county, dates from c1450. Four Cornish crosses at Basil Barton S of church.

St. Columb Major S'nt KOLL'um 6m E Newquay off A39 From patron
Major St. Columba the Virgin

Details: Believed to be an Irish maiden saint beheaded by a heathen tyrant when she refused to marry his son and renounce Christianity (see entry under Ruthvoes). Church, 14-15C, explosion in 1676, restorations 1846, 1867 and later,large handsome building has 15C tower with open passage, early roof woodwork, carved bench ends,early 14C S door, piscinas, S. chancel built by Sir John Arundell early 15C, also Arundell brasses. Cornish cusped cross in churchyard. Hurling match on Shrove Tuesday based on pagan fertility rites (casting up a silver ball in honour of the sun). Old slate hung Bishop's House, Town Hall 1848, Bank House and rectory by William White. Trewan Hall .75m NNW, built 1633 with Gothic fenestration of 1820-30. Holy well of Ruthvoes 2m S. Castle-an-Dinas 2m ESE circular fort.

St. Columb Minor S'nt koll'UM Eastern fringe of Newquay From patron,
Miner off A3058/A3059 St. Columba (see entry
above).

Details: Church, 14C 15C, restored 1889, has piscinas,bench ends,Royal Arms Charles II, slate memorials 1640. Cornish cross base in village. Holy well of St. Pedyr at Treloy 1m NW of village

St. Columb Road S'nt KOLL'um 6m SE Newquay off A392 From the railway
Road station

Details: This was built 1888 away from St. Columb Major because of threat to local business. St. Francis Church 1882.Inscribed longstone.

St. Constantine's S'nt CON'stan'tine's 3.5m W Padstow off B3276 At Constantine Bay
Church **Church** Said to be dedicated to
Constantine, King of
Dunmonia

Details: Church now in ruins. St.Constantine's well .5m North, once surrounded by seats where pilgrims could be refreshed and help bring on rain after a drought.

St. Cornelly **S'nt Cor'NELL'ee** 5.5m E Truro off A3078 From St. Cornelly.

Details: The patron saint was the Bishop of Rome until 253, when banished and martyred. Known as the patron saint of horned animals, he was also the patron saint of Carnac in Brittany, the two parishes exchanging visits. The church has close links with Gregor family at Trewarthenick. Francis,a priest at Cornelly and Creed, discovered the mineral titanium in 18C. Church,13C, 15C, restored 1886, 1900, has 13C lancet window in N nave wall, 17C pulpit,wagon roof in porch, fireplace in Gregor chapel, bust of Jane Reeves 1783.

St. Day	S'nt Day (St. Dye trad.)	2m E Redruth off B3298	From Seyntdeye, 6C Breton monk

Details: Holy Trinity Chantry Chapel in West End first recorded 1269, fell into decline after Reformation & was sold by Queen Elizabeth I, tower demolished 1798. One of the greatest pilgrimage places in medieval Cornwall. Holy Trinity Church,built 1828 Regency Gothic style by Charles Hutchins, restored 1875, 1890, 1897 & 1901,condemned 1956, repaired and opened as Interpretive Centre for St. Day and Mineral Tramways 2000. New church by Giles Blomfield built 1967 nearby. The town had its heyday during the mining boom in the area between 18C and 19C .Ancient Christmas carol, the St. Day carol, written here.

St. Dennis	S'nt DEN'is	5m NW St. Austell off B3279	From St. Denys of Paris, who was a 3C martyr (although name may be a corruption of 'dinas', a hill fort on which the church stands)

Details: Church, 700ft up, Norman and later, was rebuilt in 1847, the S arcade taken to new church at Nanpean. Ship wind-vane to 14C tower.Cornish cross. Holy well to S of church.

St. Dominick	S'nt DOM'innick	.5m SE Callington off A388	From Irish saint, Dominica

Details: She was said to have sailed up the Tamar with brother, Indract, settling at Chapel Farm. Church, 15C, restored 1873, has tower with top larger stage on lower stage corbels, 15C roof timbers, piscinas, tomb chest of 1659. Holy well and chapel of St.Indract SE of church nr Halton Quay.

St. Endellion	S'nt N'DELL'ee'un	5.5m NE Padstow on B3314	From patron St. Endelienta

Details: Believed to be a daughter of Welsh King Broccan and god-daughter of King Arthur. Said to have existed on milk from a cow which the local lord killed after it strayed on his land.On her death she asked to be buried where the cart containing her body,drawn by young cattle,stopped. This became the site of the church.A college of 6 prebends was established, and the prebends today still wear an almuce (a grey fur cope with cerise lined hood). The church,mainly 15C, restored 1877 & sensitively 1938, has wagon roofs with angels against wall plates carved by villagers in late 1930's, prebendal stalls, 14C chapel with fine altar & stoup, bench ends. Cornish cross on road to Port Quin. Holy well .5m E.

St. Enoder	S'nt EN'o'der	5.5m SE Newquay just off A30	From patron St. Enodor, whose origins are obscure

Details: Spacious church, 14C 15C,restored 1870,has wagon roofs, bench ends, pulpit reconstructed from rood screen timber. Tower rebuilt 1710. Holy well of St. Enoder NNE of church.

St. Enodoc	S'nt EN'o'dock	5m NW Wadebridge off B3314(between Rock & Polzeath)	From St. Gwinedoc

Details: She was venerated in medieval times at Bodmin Priory. Church, Norman with 13C curved spire and 15C s. chancel chapel, has rood screen, piscina, stoup, oil lamps.Church was dug out from the sands and restored 1863, 1873. Cornish cross in churchyard, where Sir John Betjeman buried.Jesus Holy Well in Rock.

St. Erme	S'nt URM	3.5m N Truro off A39	Patron was St. Hermes, 3C Roman martyr.

Details: Church,apart from 15C tower, was rebuilt in 1820 by John Foulston, has porch erected 1961 with Norman arch recovered from local farm, old roof timbers,brass 1594.

St. Erney	S'nt URN'y	4m W Saltash off A38	Named after St. Terney (see also North Hill).

Details: Church, 14C 15C, restored 1872, has E window with early Dec. tracery, commandment boards, slate memorial 1636. Ancient earthwork nearby and Holy well of St. Mark or Markwell SW of church.

St. Gluvias Church, Penryn

St. Erth   **S'nt EARTH**   1.5m W Hayle off A30 or   From patron St. Ercus
                                                B3302 on River Hayle.

<u>Details:</u> Believed to be a brother of St. Uny, although also claimed he may have been the St. Erc, converted by St. Patrick, who became Bishop of Slane,and among the group of Irish saints who came to the Hayle estuary. Church, 14C, restored 1873, has tower with grotesque figures of dogs and animals, old wagon roof, Royal Arms. Three Cornish crosses (two in churchyard). Stone bridge of 1338, widened 1816.

St. Ervan   **S'nt UR'van**   3.5m SW Padstow   Patron St. Erbyn
                                              off B3274

<u>Details:</u> Said to be the father of St. Selevan. Church later dedicated to St. Hermes, a 3C Roman martyr. Church, 13C, restored 1889,tower rebuilt 1960's, has 14C font,slate memorials 1622, 1654, 1666.

St. Eval   **S'nt EVV'l**   6m NE Newquay off   From dedication to
                                          B3276 or B3274   St. Uvelus

<u>Details:</u> Saint also revered in Brittany. Church,14C 15C, restored 1889, has tower, rebuilt in 1727 with help of Bristol merchants as landmark for shipping, wagon roofs, Elizabethan pulpit, part rood screen, bench ends, sundial on porch. Holy well NW of church.

St. Ewe   **S'nt YOU**   5m SW St. Austell   From female St. Ewa
                                          off B3287

<u>Details:</u> Church of All Saints, 13C 14C, rebuilt 1767, restored 1881, has some Norman masonry, 14C arcade,good rood screen,15c altar slab,good 18C monuments of 1737, 1785, 1813, 1821. Heligan House nearby, originally 1603, but mainly much later.

St. Gennys   **S'nt GEN(as in get)'iss** 7m SW Bude off A39   From patron
St. Genesius
Details: She was from Arles, martyred 250 AD, but also thought patron may have been a local Celtic saint. Church, Norman, 14C 15C, restored 1871, has Norman tower, arch, windows & font,bench ends in litany desk. Slate headstone 1938 in churchyard by Eric Gill.Holy well of St. Gennys SE of church.

St. George's   **S'nt George's**   1m S Looe   St. George's Island 1602
(or Looe) Island
Details: Originally Island of St. Michael(1576), but known as St. George's Island in 1602 and Looe Island in 1699. Monks'church site. Bird sanctuary.

St. Germans   **S'nt JER'muns**   5m SW Saltash on B3249   From St. Germanus.
Details: He was Bishop of Auxerre, dying 448. For 100 years there was a See of Cornwall here with the Bishop as Abbot of Secular Canons, but due to their worldly irregularities it was converted to a Priory of Regular Canons, who built the church, now the most noteworthy Norman church in Cornwall. There is a fine west door and interior scalloped capitals. Burne-Jones east window. Rysbrack monument. Port Eliot House was built on the site of the priory buildings. Old almshouses in village.

St. Gluvias   **S'nt GLUE'vee'us** in N Penryn off A39   From St. Glyviacus
Details: Said to be a Welsh priest, a brother of Cadoc and nephew of St. Petroc. Re-dedication of church 1321, re-built apart from tower 18C, restored 1883 & 1950's under Sir Ninian Comper.Brass 1485, wall monuments 1693, 1671, 1711.

St. Helen's,   **S'nt HELL'ins**   4m NW St. Mary's.   Named after
Isles of Scilly   St. Elidius,
latercorrupted to
Helen.
Details: Prehistoric settlement. Traces of Celtic monastery and later medieval church, which originally had nave, chancel & N aisle.

St. Hilary   **S'nt Hilary**   5.5m E Penzance   From St.Hilary of
off B3280   Poitiers, a 4C bishop.
Details: Church 13C 15C, destroyed by fire 1853 (except for tower & broach spire) rebuilt 1854 by William White, has early 20C paintings by local artists, such as Proctor from incumbency of the Rev. Bernard Walke 1912-32, known for his nativity play broadcast by BBC. Roman milestone. Cornish cross & inscribed stone 6C in churchyard.

St. Ingunger   **S'nt In'GUNG'er** 2.5m S Bodmin   After St. Congar,who
just off A30   had a chapel at
Lanivet.
Detail: St. Congar's well nearby.

St. Issey   **S'nt IZZY**   4m W Wadebridge   After St. Iti or Yse
on A389
Details: Joint patron saint of Mevagissey and one of the children of the Welsh King Broccan; or St. Ida, Irish Abbess. Church,14C 15C, rebuilt 1871 after collapse of tower, has 14C pieta in Lady Chapel, reredos in 14C Catacleuse stone by Master of St. Endellion, 15C west door, stoup. Holy well of St.Madoc 1.5m to NE

St. Ive   **Sint EVE**   4m NE Liskeard on A390   From St. Ive
Details: Believed to be a Persian bishop who converted pagan British in Dark Ages. Church, mainly 14C, some 15C, restored 1845, 1883, 16C tower funded by Henry Trecarrel of Lezant (see also Launceston Church), has ogee arches with elaborate crockets, piscina & triple sedilia, old wagon roofs, pulpit 1700, Royal Arms 1660.

St. Ives   **St. Ives**   off A3074   From Irish St. Ia.
(Stives locally)
Details: She was sister of St. Uny & St. Erth.She wanted to cross to Cornwall with St. Gwinear & others, but got on a leaf and arrived first. Church, 15C, restored 1854, has old roofs with painted figures, bench ends, pulpit panels, brass 1463, 15C granite font, slate slab 1642, baptistry 1956 by S.E. Dykes Bower, Madonna statue by Barbara Hepworth in memory of her son. Lantern cross. Holy well of St. Ia N of church.19C nonconformist chapels,pier by Smeaton 1770, Tate of the West, Barbara Hepworth garden, Bernard Leach pottery, museums, many art galleries, memorial garden. Feast day February. Tregenna Castle on hill, by younger Wood of Bath, now hotel. Tourist Office: The Guildhall, Street-an-Pol 01736 -796297.

St. Jidgey   **S'nt Jidg'ee?**   3m SW Wadebridge on A39   Another name for
St. Issey

Details: He was one of the 24 children of King Broccan. (See entry under St.Issey). Holy well of St.Issey near Lower St. Jidgey.

St. John   **S'nt John**   2m SW Torpoint off A374   From St. John the
Baptist

Details: Church,15C, rebuilt 1868 by William White, porch 1605, Norman N & S windows and tower.

St. Juliot   **S'nt JOOL'ee'o**   2.5m NE Boscastle   From St. Julitta
off B3263

Details: Dedicated to her in 1238. She may have been one of the children of King Broccan and patron of the chapel on the island at Tintagel. Church, wonderfully isolated,15C,restored & rebuilt including tower 1872 by Thomas Hardy,who married the rector's sister-in-law. Two Cornish crosses.Holy well of St.Juliot .25m E.

St. Just   **S'nt Just**   7m W Penzance on A3071   From St. Justus

Details: His relics are said to be enshrined in the church. (See St Just-in-Roseland below). Large church, 15C, chancel rebuilt 1834, restored 1866, has piscina, sedilia, two wall paintings remain of series, inscribed stone 6C wth Chi-Rho(X-P) monogram (one of only six - all in Cornwall). Two Cornish crosses. Holy well of St.Just N of church. Town has hotel 1813, Literary Institute 1842, Methodist Chapel 1833. Medieval playing place, fogou at Lower Boscaswell. Information: Library, Market St 01736 -788669.

St. Just   **S'nt Just**   1.5m N St. Mawes just   From ros (promontory)
-in-Roseland   **-in-ROSE'land**   off A3078   and St. Justus

Details: The saint was the son of Gerranius, King of Cornwall 520AD. Legend persists that Christ came to St. Just with his father, Joseph, a tin merchant, and talked to religious leaders. Church,in beautiful setting by creek, mixture of 13C, 14C & 15C, pews & pulpit installed by the Rev.C.W.Carlyon,rector,designer and craftsman in 1850's, restored 1872, roof bosses by local craftsmen 1990,rare double piscina,priest brass 1520. Holy well of St.Just E of church. Holy well of Roscassa 2m N.

St. Keverne   **S'nt KEV'un**   9m SE Helston at end   From patron
of B3293   St.Keveran. later
St. Achebran,

Details: St. Just is said to have taken St. Kevern's paten (metal communion plate), only giving this up after being pelted by St.Kevern with boulders, still on Tremenheverne Downs. There was a Celtic monastery at Tregoning, and at Domesday a Collegiate Church. In Middle Ages parish was granted special rights of sanctuary. Memorial to blacksmith Michael Josef an Gof, who with Thomas Flamank of Bodmin led a 1500 strong Cornish army to London in protest against taxes. Both men were hung at Tyburn. Large church, 15C, restored 1893 by Sedding, has 15C font, Jacobean pulpit, bench ends, faint wall paintings,old wood in roofs, three rood stairs, memorial window to 100 drowned in SS Mohegan 1898. Holy well W of church.

St. Kew   **S'nt Kew**   3.5m NE Wadebridge   From joint patron saints
off A39   St. Kew & brother St.
Docco from Gwent.

Details: Large church, late 14C 15C, restored 1883, has ceiled wagon roofs with bosses & angel wall plates, Elizabethan pulpit, NE window has stained glass 1469, stocks. 6C Ogham stone. Cornish cross on road between St. Kew & St. Teath at Polrode Mill. Holy well in old Rectory garden.

St. Kew   **S'nt QUEUE**   3m NW Wadebridge   A hamlet on main road,
called

Highway   **Highway**   on A39   just "Highway" in 1699.

St. Keyne   **Sint KANE**   2m S Liskeard on B3254   From patron St. Kayn

Details: She was believed to be a daughter of King Broccan, coming to Cornwall from Somerset (Keynsham), where she is reputed to have changed serpents into coils of stone or ammonites. Church, 15C, restored 1868-77, has Norman S.door detailing, 14C N aisle window.The Cornish cross which stood near the S porch was said to have been broken up and used in church restoration in 1878. Holy well of St. Keyne 1m SE, story has it that if a just-married man is the first to drink at the well he will be master for life. Corin's Magnificent Music Machines at The Old Mill.

St. Lawrence   **S'nt Lawrence**   W fringe of Bodmin on A389 From St. Lawrence
Details: The leper hospital was dedicated to St. Lawrence, a 3C Roman martyr, & later became an asylum and hospital. Part built by Foulston 1818. Now turned into fashionable flats

St. Levan   **S'nt LEVV'un**   8m SW Penzance off B3315 From patron St. Selevan
Details: He was a keen fisherman. Name is Celtic form of Solomon or Silvanus.He was part of the Cornish nobility which included St. Gerent, St. Erbyn and St. Cuby. Church, 15C, restored 1876, has good Norman font, carved rood screen, bench ends with interesting designs, pulpit 1752. Two Cornish crosses. Holy well .25m S above beach.

St. Loy   **S'nt Loy**   2.5m SE St. Buryan   From St. Dellow (1400)
off B3315

St. Mabyn   **S'nt MAY'bin**   3m E Wadebridge off A39 After patron St. Mabon.
Details: She was believed to be one of the daughters of King Broccan, and is pictured in a window at St. Neot church. Church, 15C, restored 1884, has wagon roofs & bosses, Catacleuse stone door, piscina, stocks, painting Bassano school. Cornish cross at Penwine Farm, fleur-de-lis pattern (see Washaway). Holy well of St. Mabyn or St. Paul .25m N.

St. Martin-   **S'nt Martin-**   1m N Looe on B3253   After patron St. Martin.
by-Looe   **by-Looe**
Details: A 4C Gaulish bishop from Tours. He was famous as a Roman army officer for giving a beggar half his cloak, which was preserved in a shrine. Church, 15C, restored 1882 & 1907,has Norman N door, piscina, ceiled wagon roofs, tomb chest 1590, parclose screen 1612, 17C altar rails. Holy well of St.Martin .75m S of church.

St. Martin   **S'nt Martin**   5.25m SE Helston off B3293 After patron St. Martin
-in-Meneage   **-in-M'NEEG**   of Tours (see St. Martin-
                  or M'NAYG   by-Looe above).
Details: Church built 1830 incorporating 15C tower. Holy well of Mathiana W of church.Holy well of Caer Vallack near the ancient fort of that name to NW

St. Martin   **S'nt MAR'tin's**   3m NE St. Mary's   From St. Martin of
Isles of Scilly   Tours (see entry for
                                                     St.Martin-by-Looe).
Details: Church, 1868. Dissenting Chapel of 1845. Day Mark conical tower banded red and white of 1683. At Cruthers hill, S of island, four Round Barrows.

St. Mary's   **S'nt Mary's**   on A3110   From St.Mary
Isles of Scilly
Details: Also known as Island of Ennor referring to the single land mass before sub-division after submersion. Prehistoric remains. Maypole site. Old church (Norman arch & pillar remains), extended 17C, restored 1891, only fragment of original. New Church, Hugh Town, built 1835, has wooden lion of Sir Cloudesley Shovel's flagship, wrecked 1707. Castle of Ennor, only 13C, 14C walls remain. Star Castle built 1594, in shape of eight pointed star for garrison. Ancient chambers, tombs and village on downs. Museum at Hugh Town.Information Centre: Porthcressa Bank, St. Mary's 01720 - 22536

St. Mawes   **S'nt More's**   7.5m SE Truro on A3078 From patron St.Mausa
Details: Widely venerated in Brittany, and probably a friend of St. Budoc (see entry for Budock). Castle built by Henry VIII, completed 1543. English Heritage. Holy well, 15C & site of chapel above Victory Inn, shrine and saint's chair in rock. Ferry to Falmouth. Roseland Visitor Centre, The Square. 01326-270440

St. Mawgan   **S'nt MOR'gn**   3.5m SE Helston off B3293 From patron saint
-in-Meneage   **-in-M'NEEG**   St. Mauganus
                  or M'NAYG
Details: Believed to be a Welsh missionary bishop, venerated in Brittany & friend of Cadoc and Breoc. Church, 13C 15C, restored 1894 by Sedding, has wagon roof, squint, stoup, 13C monument. Inscribed stone, SE of Trelowarren House, home of Vyvyans. Halligye Fogou, largest in Cornwall, in grounds.

Almshouse chimneys
at Tregony

St. Mawgan -in-Pydar	S'nt MOR'gun in Pydar	4m NE Newquay off A39	From St. Mauganus (see previous entry above).

Details: Church, beautifully sited, 13C 15c, restored 1861 Butterfield, has rood screen, 16C pulpit, bench ends, squint, brasses & monuments. Lantern cross. Holy well of St. James at Ball near church. Lanherne next door, Elizabethan & later was convent of Carmelite nuns. Japanese garden and bonsai nursery. Near Newquay Airport.

St. Mellion	S'nt MELL'ee'un	5m NW Saltash on A388	From patron St. Melaine

Details: He was 6C Bishop of Rennes - a person of influence,wisdom & goodness. Church, Norman, 14C, 15C, restored 1862, has wagon roofs,two piscinas, Jacobean pulpit, brass 1551 Peter Coryton & 24 children, other imposing Coryton monuments. Country and Golf Club.

St. Merryn	S'nt ME'ron (to rhyme with heron)	2.5m W Padstow on B3276	From St. Meryn

Details: Said to be the Greek St. Marina, who was taken into a monastery as a child by her father, a monk, but was never discovered and later, did 5 years pennance after being accused of fathering a child. Also thought might be the Celtic St. Meren, honoured in Wales and Brittany. Church,some Norman & 13C, 15C, restored 1887-1907 and 1962, has wagon roof with bosses, angel corbels, 15C font (from St. Constantine's Chapel), stoups, ringers'rules, Royal Arms,1617 monument.Circular base of Cornish Cross in churchyard. 1m NW Harlyn Bay Iron Age cemetery with slate cists. Holy well of St. Constantine 1.5m NW

St. Mewan	S'nt MEW'un	1.5m W St. Austell just off A390	From St. Mewen

Details: Believed to be an aristocrat of S.Wales, who founded a monastery in Brittany, related to St. Samson and close friend of St.Austell. Church,some Norman,13C, mainly 15C, restored mid 19C, has 13C piscina. Tower has remained at only two stages since Commonwealth.

St. Michael Caerhays	S'nt Michael Kar'HAYS	8m SW St. Austell off B3287	From St. Michael the Archangel and manor of Caerhays.

Details: Links with Carhaix, Finistere? Church, 15C, restored 1864, 1883, has Norman N door, piscina, angel corbel, stoup, commandment tables, 15C armour, Trevanion monuments. House, called Caerhayes Castle, 1808 by John Nash. Garden and house open to public in Spring.

St. Michael Penkevil	Sint Michael Pen'KIV'l	3m SE Truro off A390 at Tresillian	From St. Michael, with name of medieval manor, meaning 'horse's head' with 'pen' - promontory.

Details: Church, 13C, 14C, 15C, rebuilt 1962 by Street,was collegiate church with four altars 1319 -1426, one in tower has dedication stone 1261, sepulchral recess, sedilia, piscinas, reredoses, cells,altar slab, 13c coffin slabs, brasses 1497 ,1515 & 17C, memorials to Boscawen family including by Rysbrack & Nollekens. Tregothnan family seat of Boscawen family (Viscount Falmouth) nearby (see separate entry).

St. Michael's Mount	S'nt Michael's Mount	2.5m E Penzance at Marazion off A394	From St. Michael beside the sea. Cornish name 'Cara Clowse in Cowse' means 'Hoare rock in the wood'

Details: St. Michael believed to have appeared here to fishermen.Became part of pilgrim route.Celtic monastery believed from 8C - 11C, Benedictine monastery 12C, suppressed 1425, ownership then by Crown,governors and three families, finally to St. Aubyns in 1659,and National Trust involvement 1954. Castle now mixture of 15C to 20C architecture with medieval Chevy Chase Room & Strawberry Hill Gothic drawing room and boudoir. Church, 14C, 15C, restored 19C by Piers St. Aubyn, beacon known as St. Michael's Chair, 17C organ, 15C chandelier, alabasters. Cornish crosses W.side & chapel rock. Giants Holy well halfway up private drive, from Giant Cormelian or Cormoran which inhabited the Mount. Approach by tidal causeway to pier 1824 and small community with N.Trust cafe.

St. Minver	S'nt MIN'ver	3.5m NE Padstow off B3314	After St. Menfre

Details: Believed to be a daughter of King Broccan,who got rid of the Devil's attentions by throwing her comb at him.Church, 13C, 15C, restored 1873 St. Aubyn, tower & spire 1875,Norman capital,piscina,rood screen, bench ends, belfry screen,ringers rhyme, brass 1517, slate 1586 1604, 1672, Royal Arms, stocks. Cornish cross in church yard. Jesus Holy well in Rock village. Rumps cliffe castle at Rumps Point N.T.

St. Nectan's Glen	S'nt Neck'tuns Glen	2m SW Boscastle off B3263	Named after St. Nectan

Details: Said to be the eldest son of King Broccan, buried under stone basin into which waterfall cascades. He attempted to convert two robbers who stole his cows to the Christian faith, but they beheaded him bringing him martyrdom. His life was read at Hartland Abbey, Devon on his saint's day, June 17.

St. Nectan's Chapel	S'nt Neck'tuns Chapel	2m E Lostwithiel	Daughter church of St. Winnow, near Lostwithiel (see St. Nectan's Glen)

Details: Chapel,15C, lost upper tower in 1644 during Civil War, extended 1825, 1864, closed 1947, restored 1971, has porch with old woodwork and doorway, old S window Cornish cross. Another daughter church at Bridgend with chapel of ease of St. Saviour Victorian.

St. Neot   **S'nt NEE'ot**   4.75m NW Liskeard   St. Neotus's holy place.
(Nigh'ot until mid 20C)   off A38

Details: The saint, a Glastonbury monk, believed to be related to King Alfred, is said to have come to this Cornish hermitage to seek greater solitude, his relics later taken to St. Neots in Huntingdon. Many legends surround him, including the use of stags after his working bullocks were stolen. Also said to have been a shrine to St. Gueryr.Church, 15c, restored 1826, has wagon roof,groined porch, squint,slate tomb 1610, magnificent stained glass windows 15C, 16C. including stags. Cornish crosses in churchyard and Vicarage garden. Holy Well W of church famous for the cure of sick children. Carnglaze Caverns .5m S.

St. Nicholas   **S'nt Nicholas**   Oratory on N fringe   Known as The Island or
                                            of St. Ives   St. Ives Head

Details: It is dedicated to St. Nicholas, Bishop of Myra, whose relics were taken to Bari in Italy, where his miraculous aid to sailors in danger originated.

St. Pinnock   **S'nt PIN'ock**   3m SW Liskeard off A390   From St. Pinnock,
                      or Sint PIN'ick   whose origins are
                                                                      obscure

Details: Church, 15C, restored 1882, has old porch roof, unusual Norman font, 17C memorials, lychgate.

St. Piran's Church **Sint P'run's**   in Penhale Sands 2m NE   From St. Piran. The
& Oratory   **Church**   Perranporth off B3285   patronsaint of Cornish
                                                                      miners, he founded a
                                                                      church at
                                                                      Perranzabuloe in
                                                                      AD490.

Details: His background is obscure - he is said to be Cornish, or to have floated on a millstone from Ireland. He was also well known in Wales and Brittany, where he was a bishop. See under Perranzabuloe. Church remains buried in sand (see entry under Perranzabuloe) St. Piran's procession March 4.

St. Piran's Round **Sint P'run's Round** 1.5m E Perranporth   From St. Piran.
                                              on B3285

Details: Ancient playing place or arena dedicated to St.Piran (see entry under Perranzabuloe)

St. Stephen   **S'nt Stephen in**   5m W St. Austell on   After St. Stephen
-in-Brannel   **BRAN'ul**   A3058

Details: First martyr stoned to death in Jerusalem 35 AD, plus manor name,meaning crow's or bran's moor Church, some Norman, 15C, restored 1854-71 by G.Fellowes Prynne and later, has Norman S door, piscina, 17C communion rail, old wood in N roof, pulpit & desk. Cornish cross. Automobilia museum nearby.

St. Stephen   **S'nt Stephen**   N fringe of Launceston   From St. Stephen (see
-by-Launceston   **-by-Lanson**   on B3254   previous entry above).

Details: Original site of Lann- Stefan, which became Launceston. Church, some Norman, 14C 15C, restored 1883 by Hine & Odgers of Plymouth,has Norman work in N nave & chancel, south door, E wall sculpture, piscina, 13C stone coffin, 17C slate slabs. Holy well of St.Stephen .5m W of church.

St. Stephen   **S'nt Stephen**   SW fringe of Saltash   From St. Stephen (see
-by-Saltash   **-by-Salt'ASH**   off A38   above)

Details: Originally parish church,Norman work in tower base, 15C,restored 1872, has wagon roofs, tombs 1593, 1600, 1606. Gothic cross in rectory garden.

St. Teath   **S'nt Teth**   3m SW Camelford off   From patron St.Tetha
                      (to rhyme with death) A39 on B3257

Details: She was said to be one of King Broccan's many children. Anne Jeffries born here 1626, charged with witchcraft, thrown in Bodmin Jail where survived by communing with "the little people". Church,once collegiate, Norman traces, 15C, restored 1879, has remains of Norman capitals, tower arch, parts of arcades; wagon roofs, 14C font & effigy, bench ends, pulpit 1630, Jacobean choir stalls, slate memorial 1636.Tall Cornish cross.

Trewint at Five Lanes, near Altarnun where John Wesley stayed.

This house with its stone porch was where John Wesley stayed on his frequent visits to Cornwall, and from where he often preached. It belonged to stonemason Digory Isbell and his wife Elizabeth. They entertained Wesley there in 1743, and then built on an upper and lower room which Wesley and his preachers could use. On May 24 each year, John Wesley's birthday, the Wesley Ceremony is held when a celebrity is invited to preach from the doorway. The house is open to the public.

| St. Tudy | S'nt TEW'dee | 5m NE Wadebridge on A39 and B3266 | From St. Tudy |

Details: A 6C Breton Abbot, trained at monastery of St.Mawes on Ile Modez with St.Budoc & others. Doubtful if came to Cornwall, his monks probably brought Christianity here. Large church, 15C, restored 1873, has Norman carved figure, tooled stones, wagon roof, paintings (inc.16C Last Supper, copy of Flight Into Egypt by Barocci) slate memorials 1597, 1563, 1659. William Bligh of 'Bounty' fame associated with parish. Carved coped stone in church yard one of only two perfect ones in Cornwall. Cornish Cross at Trevenning Cross 1.5m NE.

| St. Uny | S'nt YOU'knee | SW fringe of Redruth in old churchtown | From St. Uny. |

Details: The saint, an Irish missionary, brother of Sts Ia and Erc,landed in Hayle estuary. Church, 18C, tower 15C, has Norman gargoyle & carved heads on tower, Tuscan arcade, pinnacled lychgate 1810, portrait of Rev John Collins, who knew Wesley. Part Celtic Cross on window ledge.

| St. Veep | S'nt VEEP | 4m SE Lostwithiel off A390, .75m from River Fowey above Penpol Creek. | From St. Vepus |

Details: Said to be St. Winnoc's aunt. Church rededicated (and reconstructed)1336 to Sts. Cirious & Julitta (believed to have been persecuted by the Romans), 14C, 15C, restored in 19C, has squint, old Purbeck marble altar stone, Georgian pulpit with carvings from Oxford college, 1520 benches, Royal Arms 1661 & 1780, unique virgin ring of six bells 1770, stocks,ashes of actor Eric Portman buried in church yard. Base of Cornish Cross in churchyard.

| St. Wenn | S'nt WHEN | 3.5m NW St. Columb Major off B3274 | From St.Wenna |

Details: Believed to be daughter of King Broccan.Church, 15C, restored 1868,tower lost upper stage in 1663 through lightning,chancel rebuilt 1823,sundial with punning inscription "Ye know not when". Holy well of St. Wenna 1m SW, Holy well of Chapel of St. Mary 1m NW.

| St. Winnolls | Sint WIN'olls | 6m W Torpoint off A374 | Origin unknown |
| St. Winnow | S'nt WIN'o | 2m S Lostwithiel off A390 on edge of River Fowey | From St. Winnoc |

Details: Name a shortened form of Winwaloe, full name survives in Gunwalloe, a friend of St. Budoc and like him played important part in Breton religious life. Church, 15C, restored 1907 with care,has Norman traces, 13C window,wagon roofs, 33 bench ends,Jacobean altar table,pulpit 1590, 16C rood screen restored 1907, 15C stained glass in E window,slate memorial 1651 with anagram. Agricultural museum.

T

| Talland Bay | TAL(as in pal) 'un BAY | 2m SW Looe off A387 | Hill brow church site or St. Talant's cove |

Details: Church has earlier dedication to St. Catherine of Alexandria, whose martyrdom included being broken on a spiked wheel (the catherine wheel). Church, 13C, 15C, restored 1848,has tower partly built into rock, three lancet windows,wagon roofs (richly carved in S aisle), squint,bench ends, choir stalls, Jacobean pulpit, tomb chest 1579,slate slab 1625 of Jane Mellow in four-poster bed with her child.

| Talskiddy | TOL'skiddy | 1m N St.Columb Major off A39 | Possibly shadowy hill brow |

| Tamar River | TAME'er River | forms border between Cornwall & Devon from Plymouth to Woolley Moor near Morwenstowe. Either from Celtic root 'tam' meaning quiet or still, or from 'tamos' meaning supreme.

Details: Applied to slow flowing rivers,as in Thames(Fr.Tam-ise).The Romans called it Tamarus. In 19C spelt Tamer. Tamar Lakes & Watersports Centre 01288 - 321712.

Trereife House, near Penzance

Tater -Du	Tatter-do	lighthouse 6m SW Penzance off B3315 off coast near Carn Silver	Little black loaf
Tean (Isles of Scilly)	TEE'an	3m NW St. Mary's	After patron saint St. Theona

Details: Prehistoric sites.Remains of early Christian chapel.

Tehidy	T'HID'ee	2m N Camborne off B3301	House of unknown name or house of rest

Details: Built for Basset family in 1734 on Tudor site to designs by Thomas Edwards. Added to 1863, sold in 1917, turned into Cornwall County Sanitorium as war memorial January 1919, burnt down month later, rebuilt 1922, now divided into apartments.Country Park.

Temple	Temple	6m NE Bodmin just off A30	From Knights Templar

Detail: The Knights owned the church (see entry under St. Catherine)

The Carracks	The KA'ricks	3.5m W St. Ives off B3306	Rocks

Detail: Also called locally Seal Island.

The Fiddler	The Fiddler	4m SW Wadebridge off A39	Standing stone
The Hurlers	The HUR'lers	4.5m N Liskeard nr Minions off B3254	From legend saying the three Early Bronze Age stone circles were men turned to stone for playing on Sunday ('men' meaning stone)

Detail: They have also been said to resemble players of the Cornish sport of hurling. Cornwall Heritage Trust.

Name	Pronunciation	Location	Meaning
The Pipers	The Pipers	4.5m sw Penzance on B3315	Said to be musicians for the Merry Maidens

Details: The Maidens, the tallest standing stones in W.Penwith, were said to have been turned to stone for dancing on the Sabbath.

Name	Pronunciation	Location	Meaning
The Rumps	The Rumps	4m N Padstow off B3314	From their shape seen from the sea. Iron age cliff castle N.T.
The Towans	The TOW'anz (tow as in cow)	1m NW Hayle off A30	Sand on seashore.
Three Burrows	Three Burrows	4m E Redruth on A30	From Old Eng. word nr Chiverton Roundabout 'beorgh' a hill or tumulus (or from 'beorgan' to shelter)

Detail: Also said to be where three old boroughs met.

Name	Pronunciation	Location	Meaning
Threemilestone	Three'MILE 'stone	3m W Truro just off A390	19C village, named from position 3 miles from Truro.
Tideford	TIDE'fud or TIDDY'ford (earlier spelling)	5.5m W Saltash on A38	Ford over River Tiddy

Details: Church dedicated to St. Luke,1845 by Wightwick. Norman font from ruined chapel of St.Luke near Bolventor. Bridge 18C, incorporates medieval work.

Name	Pronunciation	Location	Meaning
Tintagel	Tin'TAJ'l	4.25m NE Camelford on B3263	Fort of a narrow gap

Details: The fort refers to the Dark Age and earlier occupation of the headland,and the gap is the neck joining the promontory to the mainland (the village was called Trevena (pronounced Tr'VEN'na) until 1907). Castle belonged to Dukes of Cornwall. Merlin's cave. Church dedicated to St. Merteriana, Norman, 13C 15C, rood screen, bench ends, brass effigy, inscribed stone. Cornish Cross shaft in churchyard.Holy well of St. Julitta and two other wells on Island.Old Post Office, 14C manor, National Trust. Museums, including mineral & fossils and toys. Visitor Centre. 01840 - 779084.

Name	Pronunciation	Location	Meaning
Tinten	Tin'tun	5m NE Wadebridge on A39 and B3266 S of St. Tudy	Fort

Detail: Chapel by old manor house has three light 15C window.

Name	Pronunciation	Location	Meaning
Tolcarne	Tol'CARN	S fringe of Camborne off B3303	Rocky outcrop
Tolcarne	Tol'CARN	1.5m E Redruth off B3298	Rocky outcrop
Tolgullow	Tol'GULL'o	2m NE Redruth on B3298	Beacon hill
Tolgus	TOL'gus	NW fringe of Redruth off A30	Wood in a hollow

Detail: Tin streaming works. Trevithick Trust

Name	Pronunciation	Location	Meaning
Tolgus Mount	TOL'gus Mount	1m NW Redruth off A30	Next to the wood
Tol Pedn	Tol'Ped'n	2.5m SE Land's End off B3315	Holed headland

Detail: Huge funnel connected to large sea cove

Name	Pronunciation	Location	Meaning
Tolskithy	Tol'SKITH'i	W fringe of Redruth off A3047	Shadowy summit
Tolvaddon	Tol'VAD'un	NE fringe of Camborne off A30	High brow

Detail: Energy and Business park

Name	Pronunciation	Location	Meaning
Tolverne	Tol'VERN	1.5m W Philleigh off B3289 near King Harry ferry	Breast of the hill

Detail: Remains of Holy well of Tolverne and chapel

| Tonacombe | TUN'a'cum | 1m S Morwenstow church off A39 | Farm in winding valley |

Detail: Cornish cross near Tudor house is the most northern of Celtic crosses in Cornwall

| Torpoint | Tor'POINT | 2.5m S Saltash on A374 (ferry) | Rocky headland (originally Stertpoint - tail of land) |

Details: Church of St. James 1819, chancel 1885,work in 1930's under Sir Charles Nicholson, has modern screen, stained glass E window.Was chapel of ease to Antony House, made parochial 1873. Rendel Park in memory of James Rendel who designed first floating bridges at Torpoint and Saltash.

Towan	TOW'un	2.75m SW Padstow off B3276, nr St. Merryn	Sand dunes
Towan Cross	TOW'un Cross	1.5m SW St. Agnes off B3227	Sands dunes near crossroads
Towan Head	TOW'un Head	1.5m NW Newquay off A392	Sand dunes
Towednack	T'WED'neck	2.5m SW St. Ives off B3306 or B3311	From St. Winwaloe.

Details: To-Winnoc was the pet name of St.Winwalloe, patron of church (see St. Winnow). Church, 13C, 15C, 18C, restored 1870 by Sedding, built of large granite blocks, has unusual 13C chancel arch, 18C S.aisle, bench ends 1633 profiles of wardens, early altar slab, incised stone in porch.

| Townshend | TOWNS'end | 3.5m SE Hayle on B3280 | 19C Village created by Townshend family (Dukes of Leeds), who inherited Godolphin land in area. See also LEEDSTOWN |
| Trago Mills | TRAY'go Mills | 4.5m W Liskeard on A390 | Jago's farm |

Detail: Old gunpowder mills. Shopping complex.

Traboe	TRAY'bo or Trebba	2.5m W St.Keverne off B3293	Gorabo's farm
Trannack	TRAN'uck	1.5m N Helston off B3297	Branoc's farm
Trannack	TRAN'uck	3.5m W Penzance off A30/A3071	Branoc's farm
Treassowe	TRA?'a	2.5m NE Penzance on B3309	Brasou's farm, greater farm or dirty farm
Treath	TREETH	.5m E Helford off B3293	Sandy shore or ferry
Trebah	TREE'ba	1m SW Mawnan Smith (originally Trebba)	Gorabo's farm

Details: Valley garden open to public. Has beach where U.S. Infantry embarked for assault on Omaha Beach, D Day 1944. Children's play area. Visitor Centre, restaurant and art gallery.

| Trebartha | Tr'BAR'tha | 6.5m SW Launceston off B3254 | Top farm? |

Detail: Cornish cross

| Trebarwith Strand | Tr'BAR'with Strand | 4.5m NW Camelford off B3263 | Inner or middle farm |
| Trebetherick | Tr'BETH'er'rick or Tr'BED'rick | 2.5m NE Padstow off B3314 | St. Pedrek or Petrock's farm |

Detail: The saint is said to have struck a spring in the sand here on his arrival.

| Trebilcock | Tr'BIL'cock | Nr Roche | Heaps farm |
| Trebowland | Tr'BO'lun | 2.5m SE Redruth off A393 | Cattle pen farm |

Detail: Early settlement nearby

Trebudannon	Tre'bud'AN'un	1.3m SW St. Columb Major	Pedanan's farm
Trebullet	Tr'BULL'it	4m S Launceston off A388	Gap farm
	(to rhyme with gull)		

Kneeler Stone at Trecombe, near Constantine

Treburley	Tr'BURLY	4m S Launceston on A388	Borlay's farm
Treburgett	Tr'BUR'git	4m SW Camelford	Embankment farm?
Trebursye	Tr'BUR'sy	1.5m W Launceston just off A30	Burgsige's farm

Detail: House said to be by Wyattville.

Trebyan	Tr'BY'un	.5m W Lanhydrock on B3269	Small place
Trecarrel	Tr'CA'rl	4m S Launceston off A388	Carl's farm

Details: Medieval fine early hall house of Henry Trecarrel, patron of Launceston Church, detached 15C chapel. View by special appoinment only.

Tredaule	Tr'DAWL	Nr Altarnun off A30	Quiet place
Tredavoe	Tr'DAV'er or DAR'ver	1.75m SW Penzance off B3315	Gorthavo's farm
Tredethy	Tr'DEATH'ee	3m N Bodmin off B3266, above River Camel	Day farm?

Detail: former home of Prince Chula of Thailand

Tredinick	Tr'DIN'ick	.25 SE St. Mabyn off B3266	Brackeny place
Tredinnick	Tr'DIN'ick	3m NW Penzance off B3311	Small fort
Tredinnick	Tr'DIN'ick	2.5m NW Looe off B3254	Ferny place
Tredrea	Tr'DRAY	5m SW Truro just off A39	Home farm
Tredrizzick	Tr'DRISS'ick (locally Tr'DRAY'sek?)	3.5m NW Wadebridge off B3314	Brambly farm
Treen	Treen	2m SW St. Buryan on B3315	Cliff castle farm

Detail: Iron Age fort, Treryn Dnas, is nearby

| Trefew | Tr'FREW | .5m N Camelford off A39 | Farm on a slope |
| Treffry Viaduct | Tr'FRY Viaduct | 3.5m NE St. Austell off A390 | From family name meaning place on hill. |

Details: Combined viaduct/aqueduct of 1841, 100ft high with ten arches. Wooded valley.

Treffry	Tr'FRY	2.5m NE Truro just off A390	Hill farm
Trefusis	Tr'FEW'sis	Flushing, near Falmouth	Place of entrenchments
Tragadillet	Treg'a'DILL'it	2m W Launceston, just off A30	Cadwolet's farm?
Tregaminion	Treg'a'MIN'yon	3.5m NW Fowey off A3082	Commoners' farm

Details: Chapel, 1815, belonging to Rashleigh family. Two Cornish crosses.

| Tregantle | Tr'GAN'tl | 4.25m SW Saltash off B3247 | Silver stream farm |

Detail: 19C coastal defence fort nearby

Tregarland Bridge	Tr'GAR'land Bridge	2.5m N Looe off B3254 on E. Looe River	Barrow farm by a stream called Alan
Tregarne	Tr'GARN	1m N St. Keverne off B3293	Tor farm
Tregaswith	Tr'GAZ'with	1m W St.Columb Major off A3059	Thicket farm
Tregatillian	Treg'a'TILL'un	.75m E St. Columb off A39	Gathering place farm
Tregavarah	Treg'a'VERA	2m W Penzance off A3071	Streams farm
Tregavethan	Treg'a'VETH'un	3m NW Truro off A390	Fruitful farm
Tregeagle	Tr'GEE'gl or Tr'GAR'gl	3m NE Truro off A390	Dung farm
Tregeare	Tr'GEAR	8m NW Launceston off A395	Fort farm
Tregeare Rounds	Tr'GEAR Rounds	5.5m NE Wadebridge just off B3314	Fort farm

Detail: Iron Age fort on downs.

| Tregenna | Tr'GENNA | E St. Ives on A3074 | Kenna's farm |

Detail: Tregenna Castle Hotel built by John Wood of Bath in 1774.

Tregeseal	Tr'g'SEEL?	.5m N St. Just off B3306	Gath's or Catihael's farm
Tregew	Tr'goo (to rhyme with you)	1.5m E Penryn off A39	Hollow farm?
Tregidden	Tr'GID'n	2.5m NW St. Keverne off B3293	Cudynn's farm, or Hidden farm
Tregiffian	Tr'GIF'an	2.5m NE Lands End off A30	Gifyan's farm

Detail: Chambered cairn.

Tregole	Tr'GOLE	5m SW Bude off A39	Hazel farm
Tregolls	Tr'GOLLS	in NE Truro off A39	Hazel farm
Tregonetha	Treg'on'ETH'a	2.5m E St. Columb Major on B3274	Kenetha's farm
Tregonhawke	Tr'gon'AWK	2.5m SW Torpoint off B3247	Summerfield farm
Tregoniggie	Treg'en'IG'ee	NW Falmouth off A39	Reed bed farm
Tregoning Hill	Tr'GON'ing Hill	3.5m NW Helston off A394	Conan's farm

Detail: China clay discovered here 1768

| Tregony | TREG'un'i | 6.5m E Truro off A3078 on B3287 | By River Fal Rigoni's farm |

Details: Church of St. Cuby at top of village replaces parish church of St. James on moor below, abandoned 1553 from flooding. Church, dedicated to St. Cuby, who may have been born near Tregony, 14C, 15C, rebuilt 1828, restored 1899, has carved panels in pulpit, inscribed 6C stone. Holy well of St. Cuby S of church. Village has wide main street with clocktower and almshouses 1696, restored 1895. A borough from 13c, it was a busy port, with two members of Parliament until river silted up.

Tregoodwell	Tr'GOOD'well	.5m E Camelford off A39	Holt farm
Tregonna	Tr'GON'na	2m S Padstow on A389	Downs Farm
Tregoss	Tr'GOSS	3m NE Indian Queens off A30	Marsh Reeds farm
Tregothnan	Tr'GOTH'nun	3m SE Truro off A390	Stream valley place

Details: Seat of Boscawen family (Viscount Falmouth). House, Tudor foundations, rebuilt 1650, visited 1698 by Celia Fiennes, a cousin. Enlarged 1820's by William Wilkins, enlarged again 1845 by Vulliamy. Forty acre gardens created mid 19C. Tea-growing venture.

| Tregowris | Tr'GOW'rs | 1.5m NW St. Keverne off B3293 | Giantess farm |
| Tregrehan Mills | Tr'GRAY'n Mills | 1.5m NE St. Austell off A390 at Biscovey | Skin Hides farm |

Detail: Family say the name means 'place on the gravel after the stream on the west boundary'. Details: House, late Georgian by Wightwick. Gardens open to public.

Tregunna	Tr'GUN'na	1.5m NW Wadebridge off A39	Downs farm
Tregurrian	Tr'GURR'ee'un	3m NE Newquay on B3276	Not known
Tregye	Tr'GUY	3m SW Truro off B3289	Dog's farm
Trehan	Tr'HAN	2m SW Saltash off A38	Summerland farm
Trehane	Tr'HAIN	3m NE Truro off A390	Uanno's farm

Detail: Ruins of 18C house destroyed by fire

| Trehudreth | Tr'HOO'dreth | 4.5m NE Bodmin off A30 SE of Blisland | Charming farm? (huda to charm) |

Detail: Domesday manor.

| Trehudreth Downs | Tr'HOO'dreth Downs | 5.5m NE Bodmin off A30 | Near charming farm? |

Detail: Standing stones

Trekelland Bridge	Tr'KELL'un Bridge	3.5m SW Launceston by River Inney on B3254	Bridge by ravine farm
Trekenner	Tr'KEN'er	4m S Launceston off A388	Kenvor's farm
Trekenning	Tr'KEN'ing	SW fringe of St. Columb Minor off A3059	Kynan's farm
Treknow	Tr'NO	1m S Tintagel off B3263	Valley farm
Trelan	Tr'LAN	3m SW St.Keverne off B3293	Farm at church or cemetery site (from Iron Age burial site nearby)
Trelash	Tr'LASH	6m NE Camelford off A39	Farm near burial site?
Trelaske	Tr'LASK	1.5m W Looe off A387	Burnt farm
Trelassick	Tr'LASS'ick	6m NE Truro off A30	Burnt farm
Trelawne	Tr'LAWN	2m NW Looe off B3359	Melhouen's farm
Treleigh	Tr'LAY	NE fringe of Redruth off A3947	Farm by a slab or stone, or after person or manor.

Details: Church, dedicated to St. Stephen, built 1870 in 14C style, has decorative woodwork in roof, stained glass in apse.

| Treliever | Tr'LEE'ver | .75m NW Penryn off A39 | Not known |

Trelissick House, Feock

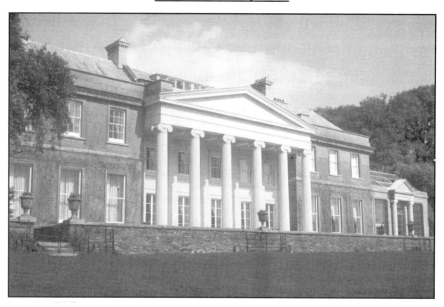

Treligga	Tr'LIGG'a	1m NW Delabole off B3314	Luga's farm?
Trelights	Tr'LIGHTS	4m N Wadebridge off B3314	Slab foot farm?
Trelill	Tr'LILL	1m NE Helston on A394	Lulla's farm. Holy well.
Trelill	Tr'LILL	4.5m NE Wadebridge off A39	Lulla's farm
Treliske	Tr'LISK	1.5m W Truro on A390	Burnt farm
Trelissick	Tr'LISS'ick (or earlier Tr'LESS'ick)	3m SE Truro on B3289	Ledick's farm.

Details: Georgian house belonging to Ralph Allen Daniell, more recently Copeland family/ National Trust. Gardens, restaurant, Cornwall Crafts Assn Gallery. Cornish cross in garden.

Trelonk	Trelonk	3m SW Tregony off A3078	Gully farm
Trelowarren	Tr'lo'WARR'en or Tr'lo'WARN	4.5m SE Helston off B3293	Lewaret's or fox's farm

Details: Seat of Vyvyans since 1427. House & garden open to public. Restaurant. Plants. Pottery. Cornwall Crafts Assn Centre. Halliggye Fogou nearby.

Trelowth	Tr'LOW'th (to rhyme with cow)	2m SW St. Austell off A390	Leueth's farm
Treluswell	Tr'LUS'wl	1.5m NW Penryn off A39	Bilberry farm?
Tremail	Tr'MALE	4m NE Camelford off A39	Mel's farm
Tremaine	Tr'MAIN	6m NW Launceston off B3254	Stones farm

Details: Isolated chapel of St. Winwaloe (see entry under Gunwalloe), Norman 16C, has damaged Norman door tympanum, windows, steps to rood loft.

Tremar	Tr'MA	2.5m NE Liskeard off B3254	Mark's farm or Mare's farm
Trematon	TREM'a'tun	1.5m SW Saltash off A38 or B2271	King's town?

Details: Castle, 13C, acquired by Duchy of Cornwall in 14C, has 13C gatehouse, castellated house added 1808 by Benjamin Tucker.

Tremeer	Tr'MERE	6.5m NE Wadebridge nr St. Tudy off A39	Great farm
Tremenheer's Gate	Tr'men'EAR's Gate	W fringe of Penzance	Longstone farm
Tremodrett	Tr'MOD'rit	5.5m NW St. Austell off A30	Modred's farm
Tremore bridge	Tr'MOOR Bridge	4m SW Bodmin off A30	Great farm or Horse's farm near bridge
Tremough	Tr'MO	1m NW Penryn off A39	Pigs' farm

Details: Original house of 1712 was until recently a Catholic School, now Falmouth School of Art/Cornwall University

Trenance	Tr'NANCE	5m NE Newquay off B3276 nr Mawgan Porth	Valley farm
Trenance	Tr'NANCE	4m SW Wadebridge off A39	Valley farm
Trenarren	Tr'NA'ren	2.5m S. St. Austell off A390	Crane's or Gerent's fort.

Details: The fort is the Iron Age cliff castle on Black Head nearby. Famous Cornish historian, A.L. Rowse, lived at Trenarren House for many years after admiring it as boy

Trencreek	Tren'CREEK	SE fringe of Newquay off A392	Farm by ancient barrow
Trencrom	Tren'CRUM	2.75m S St. Ives off A3074	Farm on the curve

Details: Probably referring to side of Trencrom Hill, known as 'hunched bulge'in 18C.Iron Age hillfort, NT.

Trendeal	Trn'DEEL	2m S Summercourt off B3275	Leafy farm by fort

Detail: Earthwork .5m N.

Trendrine	Trend'REEN	2.5m W St. Ives on B3306	Thorn bush farm
Trenear	Tr'NEAR	2.75m NE Helston on B3297	Hens' farm or Anear's farm

Detail: Poldark Mine complex.

Treneglos	Tr'NEG'loss	10.5m NW Launceston off A395	Church farm (of church of St. Gregory).

Details: Built in 12C, administered by Benedictine Priory at Tywardreath - which explains the dedication, as the saint was a Benedictine monk before becoming Pope. As teacher he promoted the liturgy, often sung, and the Gregorian Chant is named after him. Church, Norman & later, restored 1858, has Norman tympanum in S door, wagon roof in porch, stocks. In 1847 the churchwardens were arraigned before archdeacon for refusing to have the church linen laundered.

Trenethick Barton	Tr'NETH'ick Barton	1m NE Helston on B3297	Hilly place farm

Detail: Late 16C house with separate Tudor arch gatehouse and room above. Cornish cross.

Trenewan	Tr'NEW'un	5m W Looe off A387	Newyen's farm
Trengilly	Tren'GILLy	5.5m sw Falmouth nr Constantine	Grove farm

| Trengwainton | Tren'GWAIN'tun | 2m NW Penzance off A30 by pass nr Madron | Springtime farm |

Detail: Gardens open to public. Holy well of Nanceglos on road 200 yds N of main entrance. Bolitho family/National Trust.

| Trennick | TREN'ick | S fringe of Truro off A39 | Guethenoc's dwelling? |
| Trenowth | Tr'NOW'th | 5.5m SW St. Austell off A390 | New farm |

Detail: Below neo-Georgian house of 1928 are the remains of chapel mentioned in 1405.

| Trenoweth | Tr'NOW'th | 2m SW Penryn off A39 | New farm |
| Trenython | Tr'NY'thun | 2m NW Fowey off B3269 | Furze farm |

Details: House 1872 by Italian architect for Giuseppe Garibaldi, who gave it to Col. John Peard for his help in his Italian campaigns. Bishop's Palace 1891- 1906. Now hotel.

| Trequite | Tr'QUITE | 3.5m NE Wadebridge off A39 | Wood farm |
| Trereife | Treev | 1.5m SW Penzance off A30/B3317 | Reeve's or lord's farm |

Details: Manor house 18C. and earlier. Garden. Open to public.

| Trerice | Tr'RICE | 2.5m SE Newquay off A3058 | Ford farm |

Details: Exceptionally fine Elizabethan house, also has garden & Lawnmower Museum. National Trust.

Trerulefoot	Tr'ROOL'foot	6m W Saltash on A38 & A374	Major traffic intersection Meeting of three roads
Treryn Dinas	Tr'een Dye'nas	2.5m SE St. Buryan off B3315	Cliff castle farm
Tresavean	Trez'a'VEAN	2m SE Redruth off A393	Little sow's farm

Detail: Important mine workings in area.

Tresevern	Tr'SEV'ern	3.5m SE Redruth (at head of Stithians lake)	Strawberry farm?
Tresawle	Tr'SAWL	4m NE Truro off A3078	Healthy place farm
Tresco	TRESS'co	Isles of Scilly 2m NW St. Mary's	Elder trees settlement

Details: Tresco Abbey, built Augustus Smith 1831. Remains of Benedictine Priory of St. Nicholas, 13C, restored 1877-9, with inscribed stone. Sub tropical gardens, with Valhalla (figure heads etc). Remains of King Charles Castle, 1550. Replacement Cromwell's Castle 1651. Blockhouse, small fort of late 16C or early 17C.

Trescowe	Tr'SCOW (as in cow)	6m NW Helston off A394	Elder trees farm
Tresillian	Tr'ZIL'yan	2.5m NE Truro on A390	Sulyan's farm
Treskillard	Tr'KILL'ad	2.5m sw Redruth off B3297 nr Four Lanes	Kite's hill farm

Detail: Shire Horse & Carriage Museum.

| Treskinnick Cross | Tr'SKIN'ick Cross | 4.5m s Bude on A39 | Reed bed farm |
| Treslothan | Tres'LOTH'un | 1.5m S Camborne off B3303 | Place near a lake? |

Details: St. John's Chapel (to Pendarves House) 1842 by Wightwick. Interesting stones with early inscriptions, 14c alabaster panel. Pendarves Mausoleum. Cornish cross.

| Tresmeer | Trez'meer | 7m NW Launceston off A395 | Gwasmer's farm |

Details: Church, 13c dedicated to St. Winwaloe (see Gunwalloe), when rebuilt 1881 rededicated to St. Nicholas, has 13C windows, piscina, stoup. Cornish crosses.

| Tresowes | Tr'sow'is (as in cow) | 4m W Helston off A394 | Englishman's farm |

Tresparrett	Tres'PAR'et	3m E Boscastle off B3263	Middle or inner moor farm
Trestrayle	Trus'TRAIL	5m NE Truro	Straw mat farm
Tresvennack	Tress'VEN'ick	2.75m SW Penzance off A30	Strawberry land farm

Detail: Tresvennack Pillar to SW.

Treswithian	Trez'WID'yan (or Trez'JED'en)	W fringe of Camborne off A3047	Farm below a tree
Trethevy	Tr'THE'vee (earlier Tr'davy)	1.5m NE Tintagel on B3263	David's farm

Details: Inscribed stone. Holy well opposite mission church of St. Perran.

Trethevy Quoit	Tr'thee'vee' Kwoyt (earlier Tr'davy)	3m N Liskeard off B3254	Named from nearby Trethevy farm (David's farm).

Details: Megalithic chamber tomb. Known as giant's house. Cornwall Heritage Trust.

Trethorne	Tr'THORN	3m W Launceston off A30	Not known

Detail: Leisure Farm

Trethosa	Tre'THOSE'a	5m NW St. Austell off A3058	Not known
Trethowell	Tr'THOW'l (archaic Treth'OW'all)	.75m NW St. Austell on B3274 off A391 by St. Austell River	Dywel's farm
Trethurgy	Tr'THUR'gee	2.5m NE St. Austell off A391	Otter or Durgi's farm
Trevadlock	Tr'VAD'luck	5.5m SW Launceston off B3257	Aspen tree farm
Trevalga	Tr'VAL'ger	1m SW Boscastle on B3263	Broad hill or Algar's farm

Details: Church, dedicated to St. Petroc,13C, 15C, restored 1875, has old roofs, piscina, squint, reredos 16C, Cornish Cross. Village protected by Marlborough College under will of Gerald Curgenven.

Trevance	Tr'VANCE (formerly Trevantros)	2m SE Padstow on A389 (2m from St. Issey)	Hillspur farm
Trevanion	Tr'VAN'ee'un	S fringe of Wadebridge off A389	Anion's farm
Trevarno	Tr'VAR'no	2m NW Helston off B3303	Not known

Details: House 19C, gardens, National Museum of Gardening, vintage toy exhibition, craft workshops, including hand-made soap etc.

Trevarren	Tr'VAR'en	.75m N Indian Queens nr St. Columb Rd Station off A39	Merren's farm
Trevarth	Tr'VARTH	2m SE Redruth off B3298	Horse farm
Trevaunance Cove	Tr'WAR'nans Cove	.5m St. Agnes off B3285	Valley Farm by cove
Trevedra	Tr'VED'ra?	2m NE Land's End off A30	Modred's farm?
Treveighan	Tr'VAY'gun	3m SW Camelford off A39 or B3266	Little farm
Trevelgue Head	Tr'VELG' Head?	2m NE Newquay off B3276 on Porth Island	Not known

Details: Promontory fort with banks, ditches and hut circles, .25m NW two large bowl barrows, in 19C found to cover stone cists containing burials, one with stone battleaxe.

Trevellas	Tr'VEL'ez	1.5m NE St. Agnes off B3285	Angels' farm or Melyd's farm

Detail: Airfield. Birthplace of John Opie at Harmony Cottage.

Trevelmond	Tr'VEL'mund	3m SW Liskeard off A390	Mill or mineral house farm
Trevemper	Tr'VEMP'er	2.5m S Newquay off A3075	Cove farm

Treven	Tr'VEN	.5m S Tintagel on B3263	Fen farm
Trevenen	Tr'VEN'in	2m NE Helston on A394	Woman's farm
Trevenna Cross	Tr'VEN'a Cross	.5m S Mawgan in Pydar off A3059	Hill farm or monks' hill.
Treverbyn	Tr'VER'bin	3m NW St. Austell off A391	Erbin's farm

Details: Church of St. Peter, built 1850 by G.E.Street(the second church built by him in his own name, the first was at Par). Style Early Decorated, but strong and simple.

Treverbyn Bridge	Tr'VER'bin Bridge	1.5m E St. Neot off A38	Erbin's farm near Bridge

Detail: Old bridge of 1412

Treverva	Tr'VERV'a	2.5m S Penryn off A39	Urvo's farm
Trevia	TREE'v'a?	.25m NW Camelford off B3266	Weavers' farm?
Treviglas	Tr'VIG'las	NE fringe of Newquay	Church town farm
Trevigro	Tr'VIG'gro	1.5m W Callington off A390	Not known, but Nicholas Trefigerow there in 1327
Treviscoe	Tr'VIS'co	5m NW St. Austell off B3279	Otker's farm
Trevithick	Tr'VITH'ick	S fringe of Newquay on A3075	Budec's farm
Trevithick's Cottage	Tr'VITH'ick's Cottage	SW fringe of Camborne at Higher Penponds on B3303	Budoc's farm

Detail: House lived in by Richard Trevithick.National Trust

Trevoll	Tr'VOLL	2.5m S Newquay off A3058	Clay farm (near disused quarry)
Trevone	Tr'VONE	1.5m W Padstow off B3276	River farm
Trevorrick	Tr'VO'rick (short 'o')	3.5m SW Padstow off B3276	Gorec's farm
Trevose	Tr'VOZE (as in 'hose')	4m NW Padstow off B3276	Farm by bank fort

Detail: Lighthouse 1847 at Trevose Head.

Trevowhan	Tr'VOW'un? (as in 'cow')	3.5m NE St. Just on B3306	Oxen farm
Trewalder	Tr'WALL'der	2m SW Camelford off A39	Walder's or leader's farm
Trewartha	Tr'WARTH'a	7m NE St. Mawes off A3078	Upper farm
Trewan	Troon	1m N St. Columb Major off A39	Not known

Details: House built 1633 by John Vivian junior branch of Trelowarren Vyvyans. Remained in Vyvyans hands (the W. wing restored in 1850's) until sold in 1920 to Mr. Hawkey.

Trewardale	Tr'dawl?	4m NW Bodmin off A30	Meadow farm
Trewarmett	Tr'WOR'mit	1.5m SE Tintagel on B3263	Gorman's farm

Detail: 19C slate quarry and beam engine.

Trewartha	Tr'WAR'tha	1.75m E St. Agnes off B3285	Upper farm
Trewarthenick	Tr'THEN'ick (earlier Tr'DIN'ick)	5m E Truro	Gwethenek's farm.

Details: House, 1686, remodelled in 1831 by Henry Harrison (wings subsequently demolished).

Trewashford	Tr'WASHfud	5.5m NW Saltash off A388	Washing ford farm

Trewassa	**Tr'WOSS'a**	3m NE Camelford off A395	Gwasso's farm

Detail: Remains of chapel

Trewavas Head	**Tr'WAR'vis Head**	4m W Helston off A394	Winter pasture farm
Trewellard	**Tr'WELL'ard**	1.5m N St. Just on B3306	Welard's or Gwylarth's farm, or farm near mines.

Detail: Levant Mine Beam Engine.

Trewen	**Tr'WENN**	5m SW Launceston off A395	White farm

Details: Small church of St. Michael, 14C, 15C, restored 1864, has Norman font of Polyphant stone, 14C E window, stoup, granite slab to Ralph Honey 1596 in churchyard.

Trewennack	**Tr'WENN'ick**	1.5m NE Helston on A394	Weedy place farm
Trewhiddle	**Tr'WID'l**	1m SW St. Austell off B3273	Irishman's farm?
Trewidland	**Tr'WID'lund**	3m S Liskeard off B3254 or B3252	Gwethelan's or Gwydhelan's farm
Trewint	**Tr'WINT**	5.5m SW Bude off A30	Windy farm
Trewint	**Tru'WINT**	8m SW Launceston on A30	Windy farm

Detail: Isbell's Cottage where Wesley stayed (open every day, except Christmas Day).

Trewirgie	**Tr'WIRG'ee**	S fringe of Redruth	Gwlihgy's or Gwithgi's farm

Detail: Trewirgie House, 17C, later home of Thomas Haweis, founder of London Missionary Society 1795, rebuilt 1820, lived in by A.K. Hamilton Jenkin, Cornish historian, until 1980.

Trewithen	**Tr'WITH'n**	6m NE Truro off A390	Vuethen's farm or Tree Place farm

Details: 17C house, re-built in 18C by Sir Robert Taylor, aided by Thomas Edwards. E front added mid-century, and other work in 1764. Gardens and plant nursery open to public.

Trewithian	**Tr'WITH'ee'an**	3m NE St. Mawes on A3078	Gwethyen's farm
Trewollock	**Tr'WOLL'ock**	.5m N Gorran Haven off B3273	Uualoc's farm
Trewoofe	**Trove**	2m E St. Buryan off B3315	Smith's farm, Winter farm or Blackbird farm (the last being the present owner's preference from coat of arms.)
Trewoon	**TROO'un**	1.5m W St. Austell on A3058	Downs farm
Treworga	**Tr'WOR'ga**	5.5m SE Truro off A30718, near Ruan High Lanes	Low hedged farm
Treworgey	**Tr'WER'gee**	4.5m S Liskeard off B3254	Gorgi's or Wurci's farm
Trewortha	**Tr'WOR'tha**	9m N Liskeard off B3254	Upper farm

Details: Trewortha Farm Centre where Bronze Age Village on Twelve Men's Moor built from 1995

Treworthal	**Tr'WAR'thul**	4m NE St. Mawes off A3078	Marshy farm
Treyarnon	**Tr'ARN'un**	4m W Padstow off B3276	Yarnenn's farm or Little Hen farm
Trezaise	**Tr'ZAISE**	1m S Roche on B3274	Englishman's farm
Trispen	**TRISS'pn**	3.5m NE Truro on A39	Despan's farm?
Troon	**Troon**	1.5m SE Camborne off B3303 or B3280	Downland farm

Details: Holy well of St. Ia .5m W of village where chapel once stood. King Edward Mine training centre.

| Truro | **TRUR'o** (older form Trur'a) | on A39 and A390 | Obscure name Tri-berow, thought to mean three fast flowing rivers or town on slope. |

Details: Old trading port, stannary town, city from 1877. Administrative centre of Cornwall. Georgian centre. Richard Lander (explorer) monument. Cathedral (begun 1880), first new cathedral since St. Paul's rebuild. Holy well of St. Clements (not visible), Holy well of St. Dominic at St. Georges Vicarage, Holy well of St. Marin at Trehaverne, County Hall; Law Courts (prize-winning building); Royal Cornwall Museum; Hall for Cornwall. Public parks. Royal Cornwall Hospital on outskirts at Treliske. Tourist office: Municipal Building, Boscawen St. 01872 - 274555.

| Truthall | **TRUTH'l** | 1.5m NW Helston | Obscure |

Details: medieval hall house, home of William Oliver, famous for his Bath biscuits

Truthwall	**TROO'thell**	.75m N St. Just on B3306	Thicket or Wall farm
Truthwall	**TROO'el** or **Trawle**	1m NE Marazion off A394 on Red River	Judihael's farm
Tuckingmill	**TUCK'ing'mill**	1m E Camborne on A3047	Fulling mill

Details: All Saints Church 1844 in Norman style by J. Hayward. Font from St. Derwa's Chapel, Menadarva 11C.

| Tuckingmill | **TUCK'n'mill** | 1m N Helston off B3297 | Fulling mill. William Bickford invented safety fuse here. |
| Turnaware Point | **TURN'a'ware Point** | 4m SE Truro off B3289 on River Fal | Meeting of three creeks and Turnan's Weir |

Tutwell	TUT'wl	4.5m NE Callington off A388	Above River Tamar Old Eng. 'tot-oern' Look-out place or Hill view
Twelveheads	TWELVE'heads	4m SW Truro off A39/A390	Twelve headed tin stamping mill 17-19C
Twelve Men's Moor	Twelve Men's Moor	7m N Liskeard off B3254	Owned by Prior & Canons of Launceston, who had twelve tenants in 1284.
Two Burrows	Two Burrows	3.75m NW Redruth off A30	Hills or tumulus (see under Threeburrows)
Two Water's Foot	Too'WATERS'foot	4m W Liskeard on A38	Meeting of St. Neot & Fowey rivers (or Loveney)
Tywardreath	Ty'war'DRETH	4m NE St. Austell off A3082	House on the Strand

Details: Important Priory here in middle ages. Church of St. Andrews, 14C, 15C features remain after rebuild in 1880 by Richard Coad, has piscinas, bench ends, pulpit with old woodwork, alabaster reredos, tomb of Thomas Colyns, 1539, last prior of Priory. Cross to John Gott, third Bishop of Truro, who lived at Trenython Manor. Butter market 1860.

| Tywarnhale | Ty'warn'HAIL | In central Perranporth off B3285 | House on the estuary |

U

| Upton | UP'tn | 1m SW Bude off A3073 | Horses' meadow |
| Upton Cross | UP'tn Cross | 5m NE Liskeard on B3254 | Named from nearby Upton (English upp+tun) Upper or Higher Farm |

Detail: Village at crossroads, founded 1879. Lynher Valley Dairy (Cornish Yarg cheese) open to public.

V

Vale of Mawgan	Vale of MAWG'n	5m NE Newquay off A3059	From St. Mawgan in Pydar and Lanherne (church site) (see under St. Mawgan).
Valley Truckle	Valley TRUCK'l	1.5m SW Camelford on A39	Tucking mill (for treating wool)
Varfell	VAR'fl	2.5m NE Penzance off A30	High road or from Wherwell family, landowners in area
Vellan Head	Vell'n Head	8m S Helston off A3083	Mill Head or Yellow Point

Detail: Windmill Croft mile to SE

Vellanoweth	Vell'n'OW'eth (ow as in cow)	3m NE Penzance off B3309	New mill
Vellynsaundry	Vell'n'SAWN'dree	1.5m SW Camborne off B3303 near Ramsgate	Saundry's mill
Venterdon	Vent'er'DUN	3m N Callington off A388	Water, spring or shallow well

Detail: Duchy Home Farm College

| Ventongimps | Venton'GIMPS | 2m SE Perranporth off A3075 | Well or spring in flat place, or evenly flowing spring |

One of the Round Houses at Veryan

Veryan	**Very'un**	5.5m NE St. Mawes off A3078	From Seyntveryan (originally Symphorian, French martyr 2 or 3C).

<u>Detail:</u> Parish, originally Elerkey (swan place). Church, 13C, 15C, restored 1850, has doorway to W. porch with unusual capitals, rood screen, Charles I letter. Holy well of St. Symphorian opp. church. Holy well of St. Rumon 1m N of village, which is famous for five 19C thatched round houses. Trist House Garden. Carne Beacon, bronze age barrow, one of largest in England .5m S.

Victoria	**Victoria**	6m SW Bodmin on A30	From Victoria Inn, named in 1888
Vogue	**Voge**	2m E Redruth off B3298	Furnace or blowing house
Voguebeloth	**VOGE'b'loth**	2.5m NW Redruth off A3074 N. fringe of Illogan	Furnace or blowing house

W

Wadebridge (originally Wade'BRIDGE)	**Wade'bridge**	off A39	Began as Wade (a ford)

<u>Details:</u> 'bridge' added when 17 arch bridge built in 1460,with wool packs used to stabilise foundations in quicksand. Camel Trail, with link Bailey Bridge,built 1991 in TV Challenge Series with Anneka Rice.Family Adventure Park. John Betjeman Centre.Tourist Office: Town Hall,The Platt.01208-813725.

Wainhouse Corner	**Wayn'ouse Corner**	7m SW Bude on A39	Named from Old English winhus (winehouse).

| Wall | Wall | 3m E Hayle off B3302 | Wall |
| Warbstow | WARB'sto | 7m NE Camelford off A39/A395 | Named after St. Werburg |

Details: She was an Anglo-Saxon saint, daughter of King Wulfhere,who became a nun and eventually head of several religious houses. Church 15C, restored 1861, has niche with pedestal for the saint. Bury Iron Age hillfort to NW.

| Warleggan | War'LEG'un | 6m NE Bodmin off A38 | Obscure. Suggestions include Watch place, on a stone slab, or after river .5m to south |

Details: Called loneliest village in Cornwall. Known for eccentricities of the Rev. Frederick Densham, rector 1931-53, including placing cardboard figures of parishioners in pews. Church, dedicated to St. Bartholomew, Norman, 13C 15C, restored 19C, has Norman window & capital, 13C lancet window, Royal Arms Charles II, slate memorial 1618. Spire,destroyed by lightning 1818, not replaced. Cornish cross.

| Washaway | Washaway | 3m NW Bodmin on A389 | From English 'washway' - road with water channel or hollow way. |

Details: Cornish cross has unusual fleur-de-lis emblem.As the area belonged to the Priory of Bodmin, dedicated to St. Petroc and the Blessed Virgin Mary, suggested that her emblem, the fleur-de-lis, could have been selected for the crosses within the priory domains (see also cross at St. Mabyn). Church dedicated to St.Conan, associated with St. Petroc, has font thought to be one of the oldest in Cornwall (from Lanteglos -by-Camelford), fine pulpit.

Watergate Bay	Watergate Bay	2m NE Newquay off B3276	From 1813 sluice gate?
Waterloo	Waterloo	4.5m NE Bodmin off A30	named after battle?
Water-ma-Trout	Water'm'TROUT	N fringe of Helston on B3297	Wet my throat (describing a dry field)
Week St. Mary	Week Sint Mary	6m SE Bude off A39	From Old English 'wic' (settlement or village) with 'St. Mary' (patron saint of church).

Details: Used to be called St. Mary Week. Church, 14C, 15C, restored 1876-81, has wagon roofs, part roodscreen, carving in porch, slate memorial 1663, carving of hounds on W face of tower. South porch has priest's room above. Much of college, founded 16C by Thomasine Bonaventure, in nearby farmhouse.

| Wellow | Well'o | .75m off coast of Rinsey | The Welloe (from 1748). Head,Breage and A394. Possibly from gwelow (views) or gwella (the best). Best fishing ground? |
| Wendron | WEN'drun | 2.5m NE Helston | Named after female patron on B3297 saint St. Wendron or St. Gwendron |

Details: Little known about the saint. Originally Eglosiga (Siga's church). Church,14C,15C,restored 1868,has battlemented porch, piscina, sedilia, arched funeral recess, lepers'window, ringers'rules, carved screen panels, brasses 1535,1580, tablet to Canon Doble 1945, stocks, Cornish cross slab, probably earliest of its kind in Cornwall. Lychgate with parish room above. Cornish cross head in churchyard. Poldark Mine complex at Trenear. St. Wendronas well at Trelil 1.5m S. Also Holy well of Merther Uny 2m SE.Cornish Cross in old churchyard and Latin Cross on road to S.

| Wenfordbridge | WEN'fd'bridge | 1m SW St. Breward off B3266 | Fording bridge over white water? (guyn - white). |

Details: Pottery

Wellington Hotel, Boscastle

| Werrington | WERRING'tun | 2m N Launceston off B3254. | Wulfraed's farm (English) |

Details: Part of Devon until 1966. Church, dedicated to St. Martin (see entry for St. Martin-by-Looe), 18C, 19C, originally 12C,was pulled down by squire in 1742 when enlarging his mansion,has 19C chancel, room over S porch,slate on E wall thought to be for nephew of Sir Francis Drake, once squire.

| Werrington Park | WERRING'tun Park | 2m N Launceston off B3254. | Wulfaed's farm. |

Details: Land owned by King Harold's mother in 11C, then was country residence of Abbots of Tavistock until 1539. After Reformation given to Lord Russell, Earl of Bedford, who sold it 1618 to three owners, who sold to a nephew of Sir Francis Drake. He enclosed the park and built a house 1641 incorporating parts of the old manor. House bought by wealthy Welshman, Sir William Morice, whose son William moved the church and built a new house with beautiful Rococo plaster ceilings. A fire in 1974 destroyed part of the earlier buildings.

| Wesley Cottage | WES'li Cottage | 8m SW Launceston just off A30 near Altarnun | Named after the famous 18C preacher who stayed there at Trewint |

Details: The Isbells had rooms specially built on to cottage so the preacher could stay there on visits to Cornwall. Open every day, except Christmas Day.

| Westdowns | West DOWNS | 3m W Camelford on B3314 | West downs |
| West Looe | West Loo | on A387 | Little harbour (from 'loch' meaning pool of water) |

Details: St. Nicholas Church, was originally a chapel, later used as Guildhall & schoolroom, restored 1852, using timber from St. Joseph shipwreck, enlarged 1862. Market House and 15C inn. Holy well (see Looe and East Looe). Discovery Centre. 01503-262777

| West Pentire | West Pn'TYRE | 2m SW Newquay off A3075 | Headland |

West Polberro	West Pl'BERRO	in N St. Agnes off B3282	Peter's Pool
West Taphouse	West TAP'ouse	6m W Liskeard on A390	From English taphouse or alehouse, 1533.
West Tolgus	West TOLL'gus	1.75m NW Redruth off A30	Next to the wood
Wheal Basset	WEEL Bass'it	1m SW Redruth off B3297	Mine complex (wheyl) named after Basset family of Tehidy
Wheal Buller	WEEL Buller	1.5m S Redruth off B3297	Mine working (wheyl) named after family
Wheal Coates	WEEL Coats	2m SW St. Agnes off B3277	Mine working (wheyl) of 1708 named after a wood National Trust.
Wheal Dream	WEEL Dream	2m NE Helston off B3297	Mine working (wheyl) - dreaming of success?
Wheal Jane	WEEL Jane	3.5m SW Truro off A39 or A390	Mine working (wheyl) Jane's mine or cold mine
Wheal Kitty	WEEL Kitty	NE fringe of St. Agnes off B3285	Mine working (wheyl) named after Kitty
Wheal Rose	WEEL Rose	2.5m NE Redruth off A30	Mine working (wheyl) on heath
Wherrytown	WERRY'tun	S edge of Penzance	Mine working (wheyl) called Wherry Mine or Wherry Rocks?
White Cross	WHITE Cross	4.5m SE Newquay on A392	Crossroad
Whitecross	WHITE Cross	3m SW Hayle on A30	Called White Cross from the old wayside cross

Detail: Like so many Cornish crosses, it has a cross on one side of the head and a figure of Jesus on the other.

Whitecross	WHITE Cross	1.5m W Wadebridge on A39	Originally White Cross.

Details: From the old cross, the head of which is usually kept whitewashed.

Whiteford	White'fud	2m N Callington off A388	From ford on main road?

Details: Remains of Sir John Call's mansion of 1775 in home farm and cottages, stables with cupola, garden temple and bridge on Callington Road.

Whitemoor	WHITE'moor	4m NW St. Austell off B3279	White marsh (Old English hwit+mor) from 1748 in much older tinning area called Blackmoor
Whitesand Bay	WITS'an'bay	1.5m NE Land's End off A30	White sand bay
Whitsand Bay Battery	WITS'an'bay Battery	3m SW Torpoint off B3247	White sand bay (coastal defence battery)
Whitsand Bay	WITS'an'bay	3.5m SW Torpoint off B3247	Old English 'whit sond' or white sand bay
Whitstone	WITS'un	7m SE Bude on B3254	White stone from Old English 'hwit stan'.

Details: Church, dedicated to St. Nicholas and St. Anne, 15C, restored 1864 & 1882, has Norman S door, old roofs, stoup, bench ends, slate memorials 1535, 1712. Holy well nearby, stone with cross on roof & 14C statue of St. Anna, mother of St. Samson.

Widegates	WIDE'gates	3.5m NE Looe on A387	Gated road onto downs (English)

The Temple at Whiteford House, near Stoke Climsland before conversion

Widemouth Bay	WID'muth Bay	2.5m SW Bude off A39	English name (wid mutha) meaning wide gap or mouth.

Detail: There were farms at Widemouth earlier.

Wilcove	WILL'cove	.75m N Torpoint off A374 Near Cove Head on the Hamoaze	Settlement near cove?
Winnard's Perch	WIN'erds Perch	2m NE St. Columb Major on A39	From English winnard (redwing)
Withiel	WITTHY'l	6m SW Bodmin off A30	Wooded district

- see also nearby Withielgoose - or personal name Wythiel, or even Gwidhal, an Irishman.
Details: Church of St. Clement, patron saint of seafarers, 15c, re-roofed & repaired 1820, has wagon roofs in S aisle and porch, small 13C N door, font 15C, stoup, Prior Vyvyan held living 1522 - 33. Tudor rectory adjoins church. Cornish Crosses in rectory garden, in church path (base only) and 1m S at crossroads.

Woodford	Wud'fud	5.5m NE Bude off A39	Ford in a wood (English 'wudu' plus ford).
Woolley	Wool'y or WOLF'lee	9m NE Bude off A39 (.5m from Devon border)	Wolf's clearing
Wolf Rock	Wolf Rock	9m SW Land's End	In 1817 called Wolf from the howling sound of the waves breaking round it.

Detail: Earlier called The Gulfe (could be from Cornish word goelva - a lookout place).

Woon Gumpus	Woon GUMP'us or The Gump	2m NE St. Just off B3318	Level downs
Worthyvale	WORTHY'vale	1.5m N Camelford off B3266	Higher apple trees

Detail: It is said that Tennyson drew his inspiration for "Idylls of the Kings" from this mid-17C manor.

Y

Yeolmbridge	YELM'bridge	2m NW Launceston on B3254	Bridge by river meadow

Details: 14C bridge is the oldest Cornish bridge with two pointed arches of dressed stone and three chamfered ribs. Compare Yealmbridge near Plymouth named from the River Yealme.

Z

Zawn Buzz bos an	Zawn Bus and Gen Zawn	1m NW St. Just off B3306 An Gen Zawn	From Cornish 'sawean gean' chasm by the giant's abode
Zelah	ZEE'la	4.5m N Truro off A30	Dry or waterless place suggested.
Zennor	ZEN'er	4m SW St. Ives just off B3306	From patron St. Senara

Details: She was the mother of St. Budock, who was said to have been born to her in a barrel. The church was endowed by the Prior of St. Michael's Mount, the tithes later belonging to Glasney College. The legend of the mermaid who lured young men to their doom is represented in the Mermaid Chair & bench end carving in church. Church, 15C, restored 1890, has partly Norman nave, window & piscina, 13C tracery S. window, bench ends, squint, Memorial to John Davey 1891, said to be the last person to "possess any considerable knowledge of Cornish language". Cornish crosses- three in churchyard, one in Vicarage garden. Holy Well of Zennor and Chapel 1.5m W. Museum. Tinner's Arms. Zennor Quoit and Logan Stone .75m SE.

Gate at Nansloe Manor, Helston

Bibliography

A Guide to Cornish Place Names by R.Morton Nance (Federation of Old Cornwall Societies.)

An English-Cornish and Cornish-English Dictionary Edited by R.Morton Nance (The Cornish Language Board)

Antiquities of the Cornish Countryside (Tor Mark Press)

A Pilgrim's Guide to the Holy Wells of Cornwall by J.Meyrick

A Popular Dictionary of Cornish Place Names by Oliver Padel (Alison Hodge.)

A Visitor's Guide to Cornwall by Rita Tregellas Pope (Moorland Publishing Co.)

Cornish Names by T.F.G.Dexter (Oakmagic Books, Penzance)

Cornish Names for Cornish Homes by Crysten Fudge (Truran Publications)

Cornish Place Names and Language by Craig Weatherhill (Sigma Leisure)

Cornish Place Names Elements by O.J.Padel (English Place-Name Society)

County Churches - Cornwall by J.Charles Cox (George Allen & Co)

Dictionary of British Place Names by Adrian Room (Bookmart Ltd)

1000 Cornish Place Names Explained by Julyan Holmes (Tor Mark Press)

Old Cornish Crosses by Arthur G.Langdon 1896, (reprinted Cornwall Books 1988)

Signposts of the Past by Margaret Gelling (Phillimore.)

The Buildings of England - Cornwall by Nikolaus Pevsner (Penguin Books)

The Penguin Dictionary of Saints by Donald Attwater with Catherine Rachel John (Penguin Books.)

The Saints in Cornwall by Catherine Rachel John   (Tabb House)

The Place Names of West Penwith by P.A.S.Pool (Federation of Old Cornwall Societies)

Vanishing Cornwall by Daphne du Maurier (Gollancz)

What To Look For in Cornish Churches by H.Miles Brown (David and Charles)

Names For Games

Cornwall abounds in strange and unusual names. A useful occupation for children would be to see if they can find the location of the following:

Brandy Wine	America
Beggar The Boys	Bay of Biscay Farm
Bravery Cottages	Baltimore
Break My Neck Farm	Bohemia
Bottoms	Cairo
Come-to-Good	Flintshire
Dog Hole Farm	Jericho
Enquire The Way	Jollys Bottom
Labour In Vain	Little Hell
Promise Land	Ready Money
Skinner's Bottom	Snails Creep

You could give prizes to those finding them first, and additional prizes for other amusing names found.

The Author

As a journalist, the author worked on newspapers in Bath and Derby and as the editor of an international photo-feature agency in London, before moving to the West Country where she was a columnist, feature writer and news reporter on the Western Morning News. Later as a freelance she specialised in articles on houses, interiors and gardens for national magazines. She is the author of "Eccentrics in Cornwall".

Back Cover Illustrations

First Row:	Cornish Cross, Stithians churchyard	Holy well, Trelill near Helston
Second Row:	St. Thomas Street, Penryn	Trerice House, near Newquay
Third Row:	Cadgwith harbour	Fourteenth century bridge, St. Erth

116